FATHER FORCE

Changing the World
One Life at a Time

DR. PHILLIP M. DAVIS

ISBN 0-9764460-4-9
Published by HonorNet, P.O. Box 910, Sapulpa, OK 74067
For worldwide distribution.
Printed in the U.S.A.

This book is available at Christian bookstores and distributors worldwide.

Bishop Phil Davis is a leader's leader. His Kingdom vision, clarity of purpose, passionate pursuit of his calling and effective communication make him a leader other leaders seek out. The fruit of his leadership is creating a new genre of leaders developed and trained to pursue God's purposes in the 21st century.

Samuel Chand
Chancellor, Beulah Heights Bible College
Leadership Consultant
Atlanta, Georgia

Bishop Phillip M. Davis has been both friend and mentor to me. Envision Life Ministries has been a great resource for our young church. Bishop Davis' passion for the family and his pursuit to help men become godly men are the impetus for writing *The Father Force*.

André L. Blythe
Founder and Senior Pastor
Abundant Life Community Church
Alpharetta, Georgia

Bishop Davis is a tremendous asset to the kingdom of God. His visionary leadership and ability to teach/lead people from all facets of life is incredible. One can't help but learn and be impacted by his style of delivering God's Word. No matter where you are or what you are going through in life, he consistently has a timely WORD from God on his heart that he shares obediently and willingly.

Arnold Grevious
Director of Sales, JP Sports
Charlotte, North Carolina

The Father Force addresses one of the most prevalent problems of our society in a solid, biblical and intensely practical way. Taking real situations from his own life and combining them with his impressive knowledge of the Bible, Bishop Davis has written a stimulating, engaging, and helpful guide to parenting in general, and fatherhood in particular.

Bishop F. Josephus Johnson, II
Presiding Bishop
The Beth-El Fellowship of Visionary Churches
Senior Pastor, The House of the Lord
Author of *God Is Greater Than Family Mess* and
The Eight Ministries of the Holy Spirit

Bishop Davis is a man after God's heart with a vision bestowed upon him that is coupled with an enduring character and exemplary leadership skills. Through his preaching, teaching and various ministries which include radio, television, and the Internet, Bishop Davis has impacted the lives of a diverse group of thousands of people locally, nationally and internationally in his twenty-five plus years of serving. The Spirit leads Bishop Davis as God directs his path, and he is steadfast in his beliefs. Through his fellowship with The Father Force Movement for Men, Bishop Davis devotes his time and energy to impart a wealth of knowledge to God's men. He embraces, empowers and encourages men to seek the Lord first and to acknowledge our calling and purpose to save families and advance God's kingdom. Under the direction of Bishop Davis, The Father Force Movement for Men, has implemented programs and activities that extend beyond the church and into the community.

Derrick Anderson
Social Worker
Charlotte, North Carolina

Bishop Phillip M. Davis has proven to be a prophetic voice for the contemporary church. This gifted man of God has an insight concerning the past and present move of God. He is honest and transparent. He is father, not only to his family and church community, but also to the nations. The best is yet to come.

Dr. William E. Flippin
Senior Pastor
The Greater Piney Grove Baptist Church
Atlanta, Georgia

Bishop Davis truly has been a father figure in my life. He has helped me with so many day-to-day issues and concerns. He has taught me how to go about the decision-making process as a man. I have also had the opportunity to witness Bishop Davis as he mentors and gives guidance to a host of males. I personally feel that this book is long overdue and could not come from any other man of God. My life is a testament of Bishop Davis' passion to help men who are in need of direction.

Quentin Johnson
Budget Analyst
Charlotte, North Carolina

DEDICATION

This book is dedicated first and foremost to The Father and to my friend, lover, partner and mother of our children, my beautiful and darling wife, Cynthia.

To the greatest children a father could ask for, Minister R.J. Davis, a powerful preacher and his lovely wife, Kim; Ashley (Davis) Hall, my pumpkin, and her husband Jay, and the most beautiful granddaughter in the world, Jada; and to Bradley Davis, our youngest son who is simply the best.

A very special dedication I give to my mother, Mamie, who taught me to forgive and love unconditionally and to each of my siblings, Robert, Elaine, Freda (deceased), Willa, Brenda (deceased), Tony, William, and Rodney—thank you for being you.

This book is in honor of the man who was and is my role model and hero, my dad, George.

ACKNOWLEDGMENTS

My deepest thanks and most sincere appreciation to my staff and teammates who encouraged me during this process and who have endured the ups and downs of it all: Renee Carter, Gary Bonner, Michael Figgers, Sharisse Alexander, and especially to the elders, deacons, ministry leaders, and wonderful members of Nations Ford Community Church and The Community @ Rock Hill.

To my spiritual sons of the Community Church Network who have allowed me the privilege of imparting and speaking into their lives and ministries. To the men of Nations Ford Community Church, who presented many opportunities for me to put into practice my strong convictions about the negative impact of fatherless homes and what we must do now in order to change this alarming trend.

To a host of other friends, who patiently listened while I mentally prepared myself to capture my thoughts on the subject of the positive power of fatherhood.

To Ben Ferrell, Mike Staires, Mary Ellen Breitwiser, Jake Jones, and the great team at TeamBMC in Tulsa, Oklahoma.

This work would not have been possible without each of you. Thank you.

Contents

The Word of God teaches us to honor our father and mother. That is not too difficult when you have a father who is responsible and a mother who is caring. However, what happens when you grow up without a father in your home? Although you might respect and honor your mother on one hand, the feelings you have toward your father might be quite different.

A *U.S. News & World Report* feature article documented the damage done when parents divorce and children are left to cope: "Nearly two out of every five kids in America do not live with their fathers," the article reads. David Blankenhorn in his book *Fatherless America: Confronting Our Most Urgent Social Problem*, said, "Fatherlessness is the most destructive trend of our generation."

This should come as no surprise to us. God said that many, many years ago as He spoke through the prophet Malachi. *"Behold, I will send you Elijah the prophet before the coming of the great and dreadful day of the Lord. And he will turn the hearts of the fathers to the children, and the hearts of the children to their fathers, lest I come and strike the earth with a curse"* (Malachi 4:5-6).

The implication of these verses is that from God's perspective, the fundamental problem with mankind is the fatherless problem. Fatherhood is the foundation from which the family is established. Fatherhood sets in motion the order which God instituted from the beginning of creation. Everything hinges on fatherhood, the results of which can have a positive or negative impact.

The absence of fathers is linked to most of the social ills of our society—from boys with guns to girls with babies. There is no welfare system, governmental agency or court legislation that can cut the rate of poverty, crime, illegitimate births, gang violence, drug abuse, and illiteracy like a strong system of fatherhood.

I happen to be blessed with a father who took seriously his calling and responsibility as a man. This book is the heartbeat of my dad, my father and my friend. In this writing you will read of timeless truths and proven practical principles that I have literally witnessed and experienced as my father, Bishop Phillip M. Davis applied what he now writes in this book for you to read.

His heart for the family and for fathers is evident in all he does, and you will experience as I have had the privilege of experiencing, a man of great practical wisdom. I believe his insight and years of experience will greatly benefit our nation as we fight to save our families. The Father Force will revolutionize this generation and begin to bring fathers back to their God-ordained place in the family.

I share this with you because as I read the following pages, I was reminded of the many moments that my dad spent with me developing and nurturing our relationship. At times it was a mentor/mentee relationship and at other times it was a father/son relationship, or sometimes simply as friend-to-friend.

As he has taught me the basics of life, in this book you too will see those same basic principles of how to be a man, how to be responsible and accountable, how a husband and man should treat a wife and women. I learned these principles observing the way he treats my mom.

This book is filled with stories that impacted Bishop Davis' life. In his own inimitable style, he uses his personal experiences to teach and demonstrate life lessons. This is how I learned from him—more often by example than from mere words.

One of the most tragic things that can ever happen to a child is to be abandoned by his or her father. I hope that you have not been inflicted with such a father wound. But even if you have, there is still hope for you. God, your loving and kind heavenly Father, can and will restore you and reconcile you to Himself and to your earthly father.

More than anything else, my relationship with my father has been and is based on the relationship that our heavenly Father has with us. The most life-changing and meaningful moment with my father was when my dad explained to me one evening who Jesus Christ was and led me to receive Him as my personal Savior around the age of five or six years old.

Whether or not you have a great relationship with the man you call Dad, if you have not yet received the Father through a confession of faith in Jesus Christ, it will not be sufficient for you to inherit eternal life.

I have always been proud to be called the son of Bishop Phillip M. Davis, but an even greater honor is that my dad, my father, was present and it was my dad who led me to become a son of God's (the heavenly Father) (see John 1:12).

Minister R.J. Davis
Long Beach, California

I grew up in Cincinnati, Ohio, the seventh of nine children. By all outward and worldly standards we were "po." That is one step below poor. Life was typical, I suppose, for an inner-city, poverty-stricken, underprivileged black boy. I played the normal games and the typical sports one plays in the streets of an urban inner-city community.

Athletically, I was average, yet I consistently won at everything I participated in because of the God-given (although not recognized) ability to outthink and outsmart opponents. This drive to win and this ability to think through situations and see the end at the beginning seemed to come naturally, however, I later learned I had inherited it as a gift from God and from my dad.

This book is dedicated to my dad, George Anderson. He was a man who stood only 5 feet 6 inches tall and was known throughout the Cincinnati-Northern Kentucky area as *"Gypsy."* He was called Gypsy because of his sense of adventure and the fearless pioneering spirit that he expressed in everything he did. My dad was a rugged man who rode a Harley-Davidson motorcycle that was almost as tall as he. You knew when he was somewhere near because of the unmistakable aroma that penetrated his clothes from cigars mixed with grease and fumes from his bike.

While his biking buddies called him "Gypsy," the rest of his friends and coworkers called him "Shorty," but to my brothers and me, he was never "Dad" or "Daddy"—he was just George. George was not a saint by any stretch of the imagination. A staunch but nonparticipating Catholic, he was determined that his children (four of us, all boys) would get a Catholic education. My mother and George never married; however, he took full responsibility for his sons and did the best that he could in providing for our needs.

With only an eighth-grade education, George was a hustler. He loved big cars and traveling at high speeds. Never one to sit still very long, he always seemed to have another job, another business, another scheme to "make it." This is the genesis of my own spirit of entrepreneurship and my passion for winning in life.

George taught me so many lessons though he was not always aware that I was taking notes. He taught me, in his own way, what it meant to be a man. Perfect? No! Flawed? Yes! Yet, there was no one who loved his children, loved life, respected our mother and feared God any more than my dad.

Fathering comes naturally to God. The rest of us have to learn. I am thankful and proud that I learned from George.

I love you, Dad.

CHAPTER ONE

Our Father—Why Is He the Perfect Model?

"He is our heavenly model."

> One God and Father of all who is over all and through all and in all.
>
> —Ephesians 4:6 NASB

> *"Nay, the fatherhood which Scripture predicates of God is not something which God is like, but something which He essentially is. The really startling fact is this, that instead of the living fatherhood being a reflection of human fatherhood, it is human fatherhood which is an intended reflection of the divine!"*[1]

Before we can commence our unveiling of the place and power of father force in our present culture, we must ascend into a higher plane in order to discover the Source of all paternal power. As we arrive at the high mountains of all spiritual reality we discover Father. In discovering the heavenly Father we discover the definitive model for all fathers.

---

[1]J. Sidlow Baxter, *Majesty: The God You Should Know* (San Bernadino, CA, Here's Life Publishers, 1984) 169.

The divine Father stands high and above all human fathers as the representative of all that is right and good and perfect for the human father. In Him, all fathers find the example they are looking for as a replica for their lives. For those who never had an example to which they could model their lives, they can lift up their heads and look at the ultimate Father.

THE HEAVENLY FATHER

ELOHIM, YAHWEH, EL ELYON, ADONAI, JEHOVAH, EL SHADDAI—these are some of the sacred Hebraic names ascribed to the God of Israel. No other Hebrew terms elicited such awe and reverence. With the articulation of these names, God inspired the hearer to lofty contemplation of the One who created them. Yahweh's infrequent appearances in Israel's history only enhanced the mystery surrounding Him. Enshrouded in transcendent glory, unapproachable by man—very few in the annals of Jewish literature could claim to have declared that they had personally encountered the Most High God. As a result, these mysterious encounters with the Immortal God only served to increase the enigma that cloaked the Almighty.

Who could ascend to the lofty places where God dwells and return with a knowledge of the Most High? If you had indeed encountered Him, how would you describe Him? What words would best communicate His majestic presence and nature to mankind?

In the celebrated Sermon on the Mount, Jesus chose a most unusual word for God. *"Let your light shine before men in such a way that they may see your good works, and glorify your Father who is in heaven"* (Matthew 5:16 NASB).

Father? Did He say *Father?* No doubt, there was a stir among the crowd as the people asked one another if they had heard correctly. Was this a new word for the awesome God of the Jewish nation? What a strange term to use for the Almighty, the God who had thundered forth His purposes from Mount Sinai and established the Jewish people as a nation among the nations of the earth.

Throughout His ministry Jesus would consistently use the word *Father* when communicating to His listeners. In the Gospel of John, the word *Father* was recorded more than ninety times. One of the main thrusts of Jesus' mission on earth was to reconcile mankind to their Father God. The title "Father" superseded all previous revelations of Jehovah; Jesus gave it preeminence over every other designation for God. Jesus' introduction of the name "Father" created a tidal wave of a completely new understanding of the Lord God, and it inspired men to seek Him with new fervor.

It is important for us to understand that Jesus was not just looking for a word that would help man to interpret God. He was not purporting an anthropological model to explain the unexplainable Almighty. The word *Father,* in its most sublime and noble sense, is the essence of what God is and to what the human father should aspire. It is intrinsic to His nature and unique to His relationship with the creation. Out of His Father-heart mankind was birthed. He was, is, and always shall be initiator, creator, protector, lover, provider, sustainer and leader. In Him all fathers find their true significance in the community of man.

In His historic sermon in the Gospel of Matthew, Jesus used the word *Father* fifteen times.

*"But you, when you pray, go into your inner room, and when you have shut your door, pray to your **Father who is in secret**, and your Father who sees in secret will repay you."*

—Matthew 6:6 NASB
(Emphasis added)

*"Therefore do not be like them; **for your Father knows** what you need, before you ask Him."*

—Matthew 6:8 NASB
(Emphasis added)

*"Pray, then, in this way: '**Our Father who art in heaven**, hallowed be Thy name.'"*

—Matthew 6:9 NASB
(Emphasis added)

*"For if you forgive men for their transgressions, **your heavenly Father will also forgive you**."*

—Matthew 6:14 NASB
(Emphasis added)

*"Look at the birds of the air, that they do not sow, neither do they reap, nor gather into barns, and yet your **heavenly Father feeds them**. Are you not worth much more than they?"*

—Matthew 6:26 NASB
(Emphasis added)

*"For all these things the Gentiles eagerly seek; for your heavenly **Father knows that you need all these things**."*

—Matthew 6:32 NASB
(Emphasis added)

As we examine the relationship between Jesus and His Father we will uncover truths that will strengthen our view of the proper place of fathers in our world. In ancient cultures fathers have always taken a prestigious place of honor and authority. Fathers were heads of the household and looked to for support, direction and protection.

Unfortunately, we live in a time when that revered position has been denigrated and diminished by the mechanisms of the media who have belittled the role of fathers and by the failure of fathers who have marred their honored role in our society.

In order to reverse this curse we will first look at the relationship of the heavenly Father with his earthly Son. In them we will see a relationship that transcends even the highest human relationship. Their love and honor for one another will give us a model for all human fathers and their relationship with their sons.

A Son's zeal for His Father

Jesus manifested an intense passion for the Father at an early age. His parents made it their custom to go up every year to Jerusalem so they could celebrate the Feast of the Passover. The year Jesus turned twelve, the family made their customary pilgrimage to the holy city. But this time, while on their way home, they realized that their son was not with them and frantically hurried back to Jerusalem to find their missing child. For three days they searched every conceivable corner of the city. Finally, they located Him in the temple, amazingly dialoguing with the priests as their equal. His mother, who by this time was most likely exhausted from fear and worry, spoke harshly as she questioned Him about this treatment of His parents. The God/Man child turned to her and with calm perplexity asked, ... *"Why is it that you were looking for Me? Did you not know that I had to be in My Father's house?"* (Luke 2:49 NASB). The literal Greek reads, "Did you not know that I must be (busy) in the (affairs) of My Father?"

"I must be about the things of My Father." This sentiment would distinguish Jesus' ministry from beginning to end. In the heart of the Incarnate Son there was a determination and a drive to accomplish the Father's work and to reveal His ways in the short time available to Him. This passion would dominate His earthly ministry.

With perfect clarity Jesus reveals the substantive nature of the Father, and with fervent resolution He executes His divine will. From the beginning He made it His task to tear down all strongholds of deception and disillusionment concerning Father God. His very incarnate being would reflect the life qualities of His Father. His short human life stands as the watershed of mankind's history to understanding the true nature of God.

In the Upper Room, Philip made that immortal request, *"Lord, show us the Father, and it is sufficient for us." Jesus said to him, "Have I been with you so long, and yet you have not known Me, Philip? He who has seen Me has seen the Father; so how can you say, 'Show us the Father?'"* (John 14:8-9). Jesus was profoundly disappointed that Philip had not yet grasped this vital point. Philip had walked with the Master for three years. He had heard the words, seen the works, and felt the nearness of Heaven; yet he had failed to comprehend Jesus' life mission.

Jesus' relationship with His Father projects a perfect image of how all children should relate to their fathers. His obedience to His Father's will, His passionate love for His Father, and His personal reflection of His nature stand as a testimonial to all who seek to be true sons and daughters.

SON OF THE FATHER'S LOVE

And the Word became flesh, and dwelt among us, and we beheld His glory, glory as of the only begotten from the Father, full of grace and truth. …No man has seen God at any time; the only begotten God, who is in the bosom of the Father, He has explained Him.
—John 1:14-18 NASB

Jesus' passion for the Father was founded on His uniqueness as the only Son of the Father. In His pre-incarnate existence, He was the darling Son of Father God, the "apple of His eye." As the "only Son," He enjoyed a depth of relationship with His Father that was beyond the scope and comprehension of the human mind. Looking on as a spectator, John vividly depicted the intimacy of that relationship with these words: *bosom of the Father.*

The dining custom amongst the Jews of that day was not to eat sitting at a table as we do; instead, they ate while in a reclining position. The dining table was formed by placing four separate tables in the formation of a square, with cushions set on the floor around the tables. The guests would recline on their left sides on these cushions, with their feet extended. In this position, their heads would naturally rest on the bosom of the one next to them.

"In the bosom of another" was an oriental phrase used to describe a very personal and tender relationship. It denotes intimacy, friendship and affection. Jesus had an intimate knowledge of God that transcended any knowledge the Jewish leaders had. That knowledge proceeded from this most intimate place.

Jesus' fiery zeal for the Father's work burned passionately in His innermost being. As one "sent by the Father," Jesus articulated with picturesque profundity on the character of Father. With precision He detailed His Father's concealed peculiarities and demonstrated His compassionate purposes. An intimacy of knowledge was shared between the Father and His Son. With ecstatic joy the Son would disclose those secrets of Father God to the family of man.

THE FATHER LOVES THE SON

Jesus' devotion to the Father is fueled by the profound love affair that exists between Father and Son. It is clear that the Father deeply loves the Son. The Son has the full attention of the Father. "Other things" never distract Jesus. He is consistently in tune with the love the Father shows Him.

> *"The Father loves the Son, and has given all things into His hand."*
> —John 3:35 NASB

> *"For the Father loves the Son, and shows Him all things that He Himself is doing; and greater works than these will He show Him, that you may marvel."*
> —John 5:20 NASB

Because of that great love, the Father has placed the totality of His divine, eternal purpose into the hands of the Son. He trusts the Son implicitly to carry out the desires of His heart. The Father rests in His love and trust for His Son. Therefore, He pulls back the veil between the spirit realm and the physical, allowing the Son to see the work of the Father. To the deep gratification of the Father, the Son reciprocates with His own response of passionate love. The Son longs to perpetually live in the Presence of the Father, and He wholeheartedly commits Himself to the work of the Father.

THE LOVE OF A FATHER FOR HIS CHILDREN IS THE PERFECT ENVIRONMENT IN WHICH CHILDREN CAN GROW INTO THEIR ULTIMATE DESTINY.

> *This is the most basic of all our missions, the fundamental assignment of our lives: to make sure our children know that we love them. To say to each son, "I'm proud of you. You have what it takes." To let each daughter know, "How I delight in you. You are so lovely." If we get that said, and said a thousand different ways over the course of their childhood, we'll have done a pretty good job of being dads.[2]*

The power of a father's love can never be underestimated because it is in the loving atmosphere of a father's love that the air of confidence, security and destiny is breathed into every child. It is also in this love that correction and restitution find their ultimate reality.

---

[2] John Eldredge, *You Have What it Takes* (Nelson Books, 2004) 49.

A FAMILY REUNION

In Luke 15:11-32, the most famous of Jesus' stories compellingly and compassionately illustrates in a most dramatic way the loving heart of Father God. The story is traditionally called the parable of the prodigal son. This parable could be more appropriately called the parable of the loving Father. He is the key figure in the story. The story centers on His unending, fathomless love for all His sons.

The story of Adam might have been Jesus' inspiration for this tender story. Just as Adam chose to abandon his Father in the ancient garden, so the prodigal leaves his father's home. Possibly driving him was a desire to prove himself. But, in actuality, he had nothing to prove to his father. He already had his complete love and approval. But a deep-seated need for approval lies within every man and woman, and it often drives us to desperate extremes. While usually derived from a lack of some sort in our material lives, it finds its deeper source in Adam's need to "win back" Father's approval. But the ironic truth is that he already had what he so desperately sought.

The prodigal's desire to find approval took him away from the *one* place where it could be found. His father's love allowed the prodigal the freedom to search in far places. Leaving home, the son found that the farther he got away from the voice of Father's unconditional love, the stronger was the pull to a "distant country." His journey, as the story goes, eventually left him lost, lonely, loveless and digging for food in a pigsty.

Father has placed within each one of us an internal photo album that is a faithful reminder of a better place. I believe this is the *original* homesickness and is a fundamental part of the human nature. Our collective memory tells us that our true home is in the presence of Father, and He has left the light on waiting for our return.

In the midst of his despair and loneliness, the prodigal remembers. Ah yes, the marvelous power of a loving memory! There is Father who gave him everything he asked for and, though weeping, wished him well on his journey. Remembering Father and home decided it for him; he was going back. It may never be the same, but at least he would be home.

The closer the son got to home, the clearer his memories became. He could seem to see Father's face more clearly with each step he took, and his anticipation was growing. As he crested the hill upon which his home sat, he saw a figure get up from a rocker. It seemed to be peering intently in his direction. Suddenly it took off running toward him. Father! What he didn't know was that Father had been waiting every day since he had gone. Sitting on the front porch day after day, gazing longingly into the distance for his lost boy to return. As his father reached him and pulled him into a bear hug, the son started to give the speech he had so carefully prepared. "I'm not worthy… Make me as one of your servants." But his mouth was crushed into Father's shoulder, and he heard his father cry: "My son, my son, you've come home. You've come home!" No apologies requested. No recriminations given. Just, "Let's have a party!"

The scene then shifts to an encounter between the father and his eldest son. This son had no patience with or compassion for his younger brother. He was a screw-up. He had demanded and then wasted his inheritance and had dishonored the family. He needed to pay for his actions.

Watching his father's exhibition of joy over his brother's homecoming infuriated the elder son. Was his father out of his mind? How could he just take that little traitor back without requiring one single thing from him? This was crazy! After all, he was the one who had worked hard his whole life on his father's behalf. He had never sinned against the family name. He had always been a good son, always faithfully working for his father.

In this masterful story are hidden great nuggets that will assist every father, giving him wisdom in handling the different struggles through which his children sometimes walk. You will notice that Father's wisdom and love is convincingly reflected in this most unique story. How he deals with the wayward son and the jealous son offers hope and wisdom to every father seeking to relate to the different challenges within his own home.

FATHER HAS LIFE IN HIMSELF

As Father God, He is the giver and the sustainer of all life. In the garden He gave man his beginning by breathing into him the breath of His life. It is that life that authenticates man, animating the body, energizing the soul and quickening the spirit. The Father is the One who supports and gives meaning to that life. Unconscious of that sustaining power, man nevertheless finds his place in creation. Although not always aware of it, man is solely dependent upon the upholding influence of that divine life force. One word from the Father, and the flame of life can be extinguished.

Not only is the Father the source of all life, but He also is the one who infuses quality into that life. He transforms a life of mere existence into one filled with dynamic, joyful living and focused purpose. He sent His Son into the world to be the carrier of that divine life.

> *In Him was life, and the life was the light of men.*
> —John 1:4

> *"For just as the Father has life in Himself, even so He gave to the Son also to have life in Himself."*
> —John 5:26 NASB

> *"As the living Father sent Me, and I live because of the Father, so he who eats Me, he also shall live because of Me."*
> —John 6:57 NASB

> *"And this is eternal life, that they may know Thee, the only true God, and Jesus Christ whom Thou hast sent."*
> —John 17:3 NASB

A father is the source of life for his children, but this life is more than just physical life. A true father is also concerned about giving spiritual life to his children, leading them to the place where they will discover the heavenly Father who is the source of all spiritual life. Good fathers know how to connect the lives of their children to the eternal Father. They understand that they are responsible for more than just the physical life they have given their children. They are now responsible to introduce them to spiritual life.

FATHER KNOWS BEST

"For all these things the Gentiles eagerly seek; for your heavenly Father knows that you need all these things."

—Matthew 6:32 NASB

"All things have been handed over to Me by My Father; and no one knows the Son, except the Father; nor does anyone know the Father, except the Son, and anyone to whom the Son wills to reveal Him."

—Matthew 11:27 NASB

"But of that day and hour no one knows, not even the angels of heaven, nor the Son, but the Father alone."

—Matthew 24:36 NASB

"For all these things the nations of the world eagerly seek; but your Father knows that you need these things."

—Luke 12:30 NASB

"Even as the Father knows Me and I know the Father; and I lay down My life for the sheep."

—John 10:15 NASB

Jesus made it clear from the beginning that the Father knows what is best for His children. The wisdom and all-knowing power of God has been one of the inspirations for the myriad of theological expositions on the nature of the Father. We, as followers of the Son, do not search for theological explanations about God; rather, we seek the comforting security that comes from understanding that there is one who does know all things. We find solace throughout the pain and perplexities of life in the deep knowledge that our Father understands what we need before we ever articulate a prayer. Peaceful confidence is ours, for the God who sees a small bird fall from its nest has His "eye" continually upon us.

The Father, who lives outside of time, sees the end from the beginning; He has no need for conjecture or suppositions. His plans and provisions for man are not based upon a divine hunch, but upon a plan conceived before the foundations of the earth. In His perfect wisdom, Father weaves His perfect plans for His children with precision timing.

Man, on his own, does not have the benefit of the panoramic view of Father God. Instead, the eternal perspective of the one who lives outside of time as He works on behalf of His creation guides him. That is why the Scriptures tell us that, without faith, no one can hope to see the Father. With faith, we know that *because the Father knows best, the creation can be at rest!*

The heavenly Father gave human fathers as a gift to His beloved world. They would be the guides, the spiritual directors, who would be able to direct the steps of their children. Fathers know best because of the knowledge they have learned from their own experiences in life. From these experiences they can effectively direct the steps of their own children.

FATHER IS ALWAYS AT WORK

Empowered by His revelation of the Father's nature, Jesus set about establishing the Father's work. Just as the Father does not sit on the "easy chair" of His throne, directing the work of others, neither does the Son. As author Gene Edwards says, "He is a blue-collar God." Jesus passionately gave Himself to the work of the Father. His agenda was vitally linked with the will of His Father.

> *But He answered them, "My Father is working until now, and I Myself am working."*
> —John 5:17 NASB

> *Jesus therefore answered and was saying to them, "Truly, truly, I say to you, the Son can do nothing of Himself, unless it is something He sees the Father doing; for whatever the Father does, these things the Son also does in like manner. For the Father loves the Son, and shows Him all things that He Himself is doing; and greater works than these will He show Him, that you may marvel."*
> —John 5:19-20 NASB

> *Jesus answered them, "I showed you many good works from the Father; for which of them are you stoning Me?"*
> —John 10:32 NASB

> *"Do you not believe that I am in the Father, and the Father is in Me? The words that I say to you I do not speak on My own initiative, but the Father abiding in Me does His works."*
> —John 14:10 NASB

In the beginning of time, God worked for six days and rested on the seventh. The first day of man began in the rest of God. Jesus knew how to labor in the "rest" of God.

With great resolve, Jesus asserted that He did only what He saw the Father doing. To illustrate, the Father is always at work. He did not set the world in motion and then step back to remain a disinterested bystander. Father God remains actively involved in the affairs of His creation. The Scriptures are a written account of the continuous activity of God in the ongoing history of mankind.

The creative work of Father was first recorded in the book of Genesis. With an artistic exhibition of sovereign action, He formed a world that was to be the living stage for expressing His will and nature in a time/space continuum. Man was the being created to occupy the center of that stage as the object and source of the Father's compassionate work.

The Father is always looking for fathers who will cooperate with Him in the divine work. The key to true spiritual ministry *with fruit that remains* is to perceive what God is doing in the spiritual realm and then manifest it in the physical realm. Good fathers are able to see the divine work of the heavenly Father and what He wants to do in and through the human family.

> *"If I do not do the works of My Father, do not believe Me; but if I do them, though you do not believe Me, believe the works, that you may know and understand that the Father is in Me, and I in the Father."*
> —John 10:37-38 NASB

Jesus' works were living testimonials to the active work of the Father and to the union that existed between Father and Son. No man can do the works that Jesus did unless he is empowered by the Father to do these works. During His final days, while with His disciples, Jesus promised those budding apostles that they would do not only the works they had witnessed Him doing, but even greater acts because He was going to be with the Father and would intercede for them.

> *"Truly, truly, I say to you, he who believes in Me, the works that I do shall he do also; and greater works than these shall he do; because I go to the Father."*
> —John 14:12 NASB

Our heavenly Father is looking for earthly fathers who will carry out His work in the lives of their children. The father's work is an example to his own children of the work of the heavenly Father. His great work is to train his children in the ways of the Father God and to help them discover the path that the Father has designed for them to travel.

This is *the father force*, a power more potent than anything designed by the ingenuity of man. It is the influence that a man produces within his own community, inside the greater community of man. Within his community, called a family, he has the authority and the responsibility of empowering and educating his family so they can fulfill their own divine destiny and transform their space in this world. He has the force of fatherhood to propel his family into a future that is filled with the blessings of God. He has the force of fatherhood to direct his family to advance God's kingdom and to reflect God's glory. This is the way of Father. This is *the father force!*

FATHER REFLECTIONS

1. *Why do you feel it is often so difficult for men to refer to God and see God as Father?*

2. *In what ways is your life a reflection of the father-son relationship you have with your dad?*

3. *What memory, hardship or failure keeps you from resting in the bosom of the Father?*

4. *How have we as a society strayed from presenting God's model of fatherhood?*

5. *What is the Father God calling you to carry out for His family and yours?*

CHAPTER TWO

Father—Why Do We Need Him So Desperately?

"He is our foundation."

> *One father is more than a hundred Schoolmasters.*
> —George Herbert, 17th century

What is a father? When that question was posed to a seven-year-old boy, he replied, *"A father is a man who has pictures in his wallet where he used to have money."*

A ten-year-old girl offered this comment, *"A father is a man whose lap you can jump in and who will keep you from mother when she is angry."*

He is a mender of toys and a leader of boys. He is a changer of fuses and a healer of bruises. A father is a mover of couches and a bandage for ouches. He is a hanger of screens and a counselor to teens. A father is a pounder of nails and a teller of tales. He is a dryer of dishes and a fulfiller of wishes.

The meaning of a father to his child is always shifting and changing as the child grows older:

At age   4 – "My daddy can do anything!"

At age   7 – "My dad knows a lot…a whole lot."

At age 10 – "My dad does not know quite everything."

At age 13 – "Oh yeah, I know Dad does not know this."

At age 16 – "Dad? He is old and out of date."

At age 21 – "That man is totally out of it."

At age 25 – "Dad knows a little bit about it—but not much."

At age 30 – "I need to find out what Dad thinks about it."

At age 35 – "Well, before we decide, we'd better check with Dad to get his thoughts first."

At age 45 – "What would Dad do in this situation?"

At age 55 – "My dad knew literally everything."

At age 65 – "I wish I could talk this over with Dad."

WE NEED FATHERS!

No matter how old you get, I am convinced that the key to a well-adjusted fulfilling life is the relationship you have or have had with your father. Fathers are critical to the security, the salvation and the stability of the world as we know it. I will go so far as to say that fathers hold the key to the spiritual revival, the moral renewal, the economic empowerment and the social sanity that we need in our culture and society for the future of mankind. Fathers are the force that can literally transform our world!

Fathers are a masterpiece of the heavenly design. However fathers are not born, they are made. It is true that men are born with the natural instincts to be a father, but the ability to effectively and consistently perform their function in society can only be developed in the crucible of life. *"Men grow into fathers and fathering is a very important stage in their development"* (David Gottesman). Their development into this primary role within the community is critical to the quality of life of the community, because upon the shoulders of fathers are the foundations of the community.

It is not that mothers and women are not important. I, for one, would not be where I am today had it not been for the tenacious and persistent prayers of a faithful and devoted mother. My mother taught me valuable and lifelong lessons that I shall never forget.

However, the fact is that when we study God's purpose and God's design we will discover that fathers are the key to every issue, every problem and every challenge in the world throughout the history of mankind. Fathers were designed by the heavenly Father to be creators just like their Maker. They were made with the instinct to create, design, solve and resolve, invent and prevent. *"You know, fathers just have a way of putting everything together"* (Erika Cosby, daughter of Bill Cosby).

I want to say a word to fathers, whether you are a biological father, an adoptive father, a stepfather, or a surrogate father—you are vital and essential to the fulfillment of God's divine plan and purpose.

George was not athletic at all. He liked baseball and watched it regularly on our black and white Motorola. We loved watching the Cincinnati Reds together. But since George was not athletically inclined, I didn't know how he would respond when I told him that I wanted to play baseball. But rather than discourage me because of his inabilities, he encouraged me to give my very best. He even took me to the Boy's Club and introduced me to the coach of a team sponsored by Wilson's Dairy. Because of his Saturday work schedule George did not make it to many of my little league baseball games, but that did not stop me from running to the used car lot where he worked as a mechanic after each game

FATHERS, YOU ARE THE FOUNDATION UPON WHICH ALL OF LIFE AND SOCIETY ARE ESTABLISHED AND BUILT.

to let him see me in my uniform. I was truly blessed that George took me to a man (the coach) who could teach me to do what he could not teach me…a sort of surrogate father.

There is an eerie cry ringing throughout the earth for fathers. All of creation is groaning for the manifestation of fathers. Romans 8:19 says that all creation groans and earnestly awaits the revealing of the sons of God. People are longing for a relationship and connection with their fathers that are both fulfilling and genuine. The entire created order is longing for the fathers of our societies to reveal themselves as the true "sons of God" and lead in the transformation of our world. And although you may not be a biological father, you still have within you the divinely created force of fatherhood. Society, young men and young women in single parent homes are all groaning for the father force that resides within each of us as men.

THE IMPORTANCE OF FATHERS

And he shall turn the heart of the fathers to the children, and the heart of the children to their fathers, lest I come and smite the earth with a curse.
—Malachi 4:6 KJV

Fathers are so vitally important to the well-being of society that God Himself speaks of the necessity of fathers turning their hearts toward their children and the importance of children turning their hearts to their fathers. God spoke of the urgency of fathers turning their hearts to their children just before He went silent for 400 years. It is the last verse of the Old Testament—the last words we read before the coming of the Father's Son, Jesus!

Why would God make this the last thing He says to Israel before the coming of the Lord Jesus? Why is this the final thing that God leaves with His people for over 400 years?

Why is God longing for the hearts of the fathers to be turned to their children and the hearts of the children to be turned toward their fathers? What is it about the hearts of fathers and the children being linked together that is so important in the mind of God that God is willing to curse and destroy the earth if it does not happen, yet spare and bless the earth if it does happen?

Why is this so vital…that God would go to such lengths as to send Elijah the prophet back to warn us, to prepare us and even to promise us deliverance from the curse if we obey?

God is placing so much emphasis on fathers and their hearts being turned to their children and the hearts of the children being turned toward their fathers because His heart, as our loving heavenly Father, is toward us, His children. God wants every father to be the foundation upon which the family and society is built. It is God's purpose that every father represents Him. He wants fathers to imitate Him and bring glory to Him. God's desire is to have fathers be the reflection of who He is in the lives of children and the world today.

The heavenly Father has chosen to reflect His nature through human fathers. This reflection is most glorious when the heart of the father is turned toward his children and the children's hearts are turned toward the father. This unity of heart will bring the blessing of heaven upon the earth, and the father is the key to this heavenly blessing.

THE FATHER IS THE KEY TO BLESSING OR DEFEAT

Malachi goes on to say that if the relationship between fathers and children is not healed, a curse will come upon the earth. God is saying that unless the fathers turn their hearts toward their children, the children will not turn their hearts toward their fathers; and because neither has turned (repented), we will see a day when destruction will come.

The discord in the family leads to discord in the community. Discord in the community leads to discord in the nation, and discord among nations leads to disharmony in our world.

I would suggest to you that we are not very far from this day. I suggest that as fathers, we must see the critical role we play in bringing a blessing to our world. We must recommit ourselves to the task of turning our children's hearts toward us. We must focus on this issue more than on our careers, our cars, our money, our hobbies, sports, politics, fame, fortune or any ambition in life. None of these will matter if we lose our children and thus lose our world. The Bible says that *a good man leaves an inheritance to his children's children* (Proverbs 13:22). The heritage that we must leave with them is both a material heritage and a spiritual heritage.

We must turn our hearts toward raising our sons and daughters. Our hearts as fathers must be focused on the welfare, the care, the protection and the provisions of our children and our children's children. Until we as fathers heed this call, we will continue to see twelve, thirteen, and fourteen-year-olds having babies. We will continue to see ten-year-olds becoming cold-blooded murderers, young boys and girls out of control, drugs ruining their lives, and gang members and other evil influences having more control over their lives than we do. The Bible says, when men do not stand up and lead, their children will rule over them (see Isaiah 3:4).

We do not have the luxury of hoping that the church, the schools or some other institution will raise our children to fear and worship God! Fathers, that is our calling; that is our responsibility and that is our obligation and our role, and unless we do it—sorrow and shame will be our inheritance.

Whether we are talking about a natural father or a spiritual father, it is critical that we understand that fathers and men with the spirit of fatherhood *hold the key to the nations*—and it is obvious that the nations of the world are in crisis.

It is critical that we all understand God's identity and God's plan for fathers. This means that whether we are talking about spiritual fathers or natural fathers—understanding and accepting God's plan and God's identity for fathers is the key to reestablishing order and stability in society, our homes, our churches, our community, our nation and in the world.

REVERSING THE CURSE

The major problem is that men—regardless of race, creed, color or national origin—don't have a clear understanding of the purpose and power of fatherhood. The average man is confused about his manhood, masculinity, sexuality and fatherhood.

> *The tragedy, or the blessing, is that we tend to raise our children the way we were raised. The end result of what has been done to us is more than what has been said to us. If we grew up without a heart connection to our fathers, we'll battle a seemingly irresistible inclination to be disconnected from our children. We need God to connect our hearts to our children.*[3]

---

[3] Crawford W. Loritts Jr., *Never Walk Away*, (Chicago, Moody Press, 1997) 26.

Due to a lack of role models, the absence of strong men in their lives or because of the cultural changes of society, many men are suffering from a loss of identity and a loss of godly purpose. The consequences for the family, the community, the church and even the nations are devastating and far-reaching.

Many young boys with absentee fathers—missing either physically or emotionally—are walking in quicksand or sinking in life instead of standing on the shoulders of their fathers and on their solid foundation. These young boys, and many young girls, are trying to find a foundation for their lives, but they have mud all over them because there is just no place where they can stand on solid ground. Their foundations are missing. So when they grow up, they will try to become foundations themselves. The only problem is, that they were never shown what a true foundation really is.

The challenge is for every father to rise up and become a strong foundation. We need fathers who will stand with their wives, stand with their children and be there as a stabilizer in our homes and communities. We need fathers whose families will feel secure in their strength.

It doesn't matter what your father was, or what your relationship with your father was like—you can become a strong foundation today by becoming the man or woman God created you to be by understanding the nature of fatherhood. You can reverse the curse that has come on this culture. You can rebuild the ancient ruins and establish a new foundation for future generations.

We must understand the spirit of fatherhood. This goes beyond the fact of being a biological father—it goes to the very heart of God. To understand the spirit of fatherhood, one must recognize that the Bible is written from a Hebrew perspective of family and fatherhood. Hebrew life revolved around fathers and their authority, accountability and responsibilities.

In Hebrew life the father was the foundation, and a well-adjusted family that was respected in society was one where the father inspired, protected, made provisions for and gave direction to his family. This is the foundation for a new generation.

FATHERS ARE THE FOUNDATION

Society offers us many opinions of what a father should be, but the Lord's purpose is the only one that counts—it is the only purpose and plan that will lead to fulfillment and destiny. The Scripture teaches us that there are many plans in a man's heart, but it is the Lord's purpose that shall stand (see Proverbs 19:21).

God created man in His image and after His likeness— placing man in two physical "bodies" called male and female—to have dominion, to rule over, and to influence the planet earth. God created "man" the spirit both male and female. Although man—the spirit (male and female)—was created in the image of God, He did not create them without order or without purpose.

In Genesis 1:27 we see the divine plan as the order in which the male was created. In this scripture we discover the clue to man's reason for being. Why did God make the male first? It was not because the male was or is better, but because of God's divine plan and His purpose.

Only the male came directly from the earth, and I believe this is because the male was designed by God to be the foundation of the human family. The woman came out of the man, rather than coming out of the earth, because she was designed to rest on the man—to have the male as her support. Often we hear that *the family is the foundation of society*. It is true that the family is the important, adhesive ingredient that holds things together, but God did not start to build earthly society with a family. He began with one person—He began with the male. He began with fathers. Man was the starting point of the future families that would populate Father's world. Man was created to be the progenitor, a creator, and a father to the future plans of his heavenly Father.

> *What is a man for? If you know what something is designed to do, then you know its purpose in life. A retriever loves water, a lion loves the hunt, a hawk loves to soar. It's what they've been made for. Desire reveals design, and design reveals destiny...Adam and all his sons after him are given an incredible mission: rule and subdue, be fruitful and multiply.*[4]

God knew exactly what He was doing. *He planned everything before He began to create anything.* When He started digging the foundation, He knew exactly what He wanted and what the complete picture would look like. All creation began in the mind of the Maker. His creation is a reflection of His thoughts and plans. Before the first ticking of time, He created a plan and He devised a creature that

---

[4] John Eldredge, *Wild at Heart* (Nashville, TN, Thomas Nelson Publishers, 2001) 48.

would fulfill that plan. He had to start with a foundation upon which to build His new world.

When He began to build the human race, He began by laying the foundation of the male. God placed males at the bottom of the entire building of humanity. If the males don't learn what it means to be a strong foundation in God, then society, culture, our families, our communities, our churches and nations are sunk. When the man, the father, the male, leaves home, when he neglects his responsibilities, or when he is ignorant of who he is, you will have a house built on sinking sand.

MEN, THIS IS OUR HOUR. GOD IS CALLING US TO BECOME REFORMERS IN A CULTURE THAT NEEDS REFORMING. THIS IS THE TIME FOR THE FATHER FORCE TO EMPOWER AND IMPACT OUR CULTURE AND COMMUNITIES.

Although we have many godly, strong, Holy Ghost-filled, powerful, praying, intelligent and capable mothers, there are some things that Momma cannot give you. Your mother cannot give you the things that the foundation gives because she is not designed to be the foundation. When a father or a male has cracks and develops faults in the substructure (the character) of his life, then the whole building, the whole family, the community, the church and the nation are on shaky ground.

This is the day and time that you are being called by God and challenged by the devil to get yourself on solid ground. As you go—so goes your family, society and the world. Take a look around at the condition of our societies and nations around the world. *How would you say we are doing?*

Our culture is in chaos and crisis because the foundation—fatherhood—has become sandy, weak, uncertain, and unstable. We cannot build a human race on a foundation that is full of sand. A foundation is always measured by how much weight can be placed on it.

God is calling fathers to live like the foundations we were created to be. Foundations are not always in the limelight, but are most often hidden, doing their job of upholding everything placed upon it without recognition and fanfare. However, the work that we do, as fathers, will rarely be seen or appreciated by the crowds, but our hidden presence in the substructures of our lives will build a solid future for our world.

Jean Paul Richter said, *"The words that a father speaks to his children in the privacy of home are not heard by the world, but, as in whispering-galleries, they are clearly heard at the end and by posterity."*

There is no value ceiling on the time we give and the investments we make in our children. It is no secret. Fathers need to just be there and need to keep their homes steady, secure, stable and safe. Our wives and children need to know they can always lean on us and know that we are not going to crack under the pressure. As fathers, we have been strategically placed into Father's world for a peculiar purpose.

FATHER—VISIONARY AND LEADER

God set the male in the Garden of Eden—a particular place for a particular purpose. God set the man in the environment in which he was supposed to remain in order to fulfill his reason for being.

The name of that particular place was called the Garden of Eden. *Eden* comes from the Hebrew word meaning "delicate, delight or pleasure." The word for *garden* means "an enclosure" or "something fenced in." You must understand that this was no ordinary garden. Everything that was influencing heaven would have divine impact upon this place. God placed man in an environment that represented the glory of heaven. It was God's incubator for His new children, His new offspring created in His image and after His likeness.

The reason God placed the male in the garden was so that he, the man, could continually be in the presence of God. He could walk and talk with the Lord in the cool of the day. He could hear the voice of God and commune with Him, fellowship with Him and be at one with God always. From that place in the presence of God he would be able to see and lead. He would be a visionary and a leader, representing Father's heart and will.

God never intended for Adam to move from or leave the garden. He intended for the garden to expand and cover all of the earth. God wanted Adam to take the presence of the garden and spread it throughout the world. This is the meaning of the command for Adam to *have dominion over the earth*. Even though this plan suffered a little setback, it has not changed. We are to advance the kingdom of God throughout the entire earth today. Isaiah 11:9 says, *"...the earth shall be full of the knowledge of the Lord, as the waters cover the sea."*

God gave the male this vision of what the world should look like and what the world should be like under his leadership and authority. God transferred the authority to Adam in Genesis 2:15, 19-20. Therefore, Adam, the male who had been given the vision and the authority, was placed in the position of leader. He was to carry out the plan of God to extend and enclose the entire earth with His garden of delight and pleasure.

It is clear that Adam was not going to carry out this plan alone. He was given a helper created by the hand of God. God created woman out of man and gave her to the man as his helper; not as his slave, not as his unequal partner, but as his equal partner in fulfilling the vision of God for mankind.

God positioned the man as the leader. In Genesis 3:9, after they fell in sin through their disobedience, God asked Adam, "Where are you?" This is not a question of location. This is a question of position.

"Why are you out of the position that I placed you in? Why are you following your wife and not Me? Why did you get out of your position and lose sight of the vision? You are the foundation; I began with you, I talked to you, I gave you the vision and the authority to be the leader and you were to be the one who stayed in position. You should not have allowed your wife to turn and go the other way...you should not have allowed her to discuss with the serpent what I only told you. Where are you?"

Men, we must understand our position. It is to be in the presence of God at all times. It is not enough to simply come to church; we need to be in touch with God constantly, hearing His voice, listening to His commands and following His directions. If we don't, we will make the mistake that Adam made—*we will lose sight of the vision, get out of position and lose our authority to carry out God's plan.*

Men, we must stay in the presence of God—that is why God gave us Himself before He gave us anything else. Look at the first thing God gave the male—it was not a woman, it was not a job, it was not even a command. The first thing God gave us was His Presence—His breath of life and His garden of delight and pleasure.

Our position as men is to be the visionary leaders who stay in the presence of God so we can extend His garden, His delight, His will, and His kingdom throughout the entire earth. From our position in His Presence we will discover our purpose as professors, producers, providers and protectors.

FATHERS—PROFESSORS, PRODUCERS, PROVIDERS, AND PROTECTORS

Once a father understands the importance of remaining in the place of the Presence of God he will then begin to discover his purpose in God's plan.

Professor

Since God gave man the vision, the command, and the authority for carrying out His plan, it is natural that he will have to communicate that plan to the woman and her future offspring. He will be responsible for accurately and effectively conveying the intricacies of Father's will. As fathers, a part of our priestly role is to teach our children the will and ways of God. We have been entrusted with the Word of God, and it is our place to make sure that our family hears and obeys that Word.

It is important that fathers do not simply leave the instruction of their children to their teachers or their pastors.

Certainly, teachers and pastors play important roles in the academic and spiritual instruction of our children, but this instruction should not be a substitute for the important role that a father plays in the practical instruction he can supply to his children.

Producer

Since God gave man the ability to lead, God gave man the ability and the responsibility of reproducing after his kind. God wants the man to be productive and to tend the garden. Men, we are to be producers—productive men who increase, reproduce and cause the advancement of God's kingdom. As God was a Creator, so we are to create through our work. Our work is the means of manifesting our purpose.

We are to synchronize our lives with the will of God everywhere we go. We are to produce the presence of God in every place. We are to replenish the earth, to fill it with good things, great things and those things that will reflect the delightful presence of God.

Provider

God gave man the position of visionary leadership, with the authority to carry out His plan. Since God brought the woman out of the man, man is responsible for caring for the gift Father has given Him—the woman. It stands to reason that a part of the purpose of man is to provide for the family.

The Bible teaches that if I do not provide for my own household, I have denied the faith and I am worse than an infidel, or literally, God sees me as an unbeliever (see 1

Timothy 5:8). Man's work is a reflection of his creative ability. That ability to work creates resources through which he will be able to provide for the needs of his family. God has uniquely gifted him in this way. Men, we are created to be the providers of everything good, healthy and beneficial for our children, our wives, our communities and our churches.

Protector

God's purpose is for the male to be the primary protector of his family and environment. When Satan tempted and deceived Eve, God asked Adam about the situation. Why? Adam was the protector. Adam was the one who was not supposed to allow any hurt, harm or danger to come into the garden. God told Adam to tend and keep it. Tend and maintain it; tend and make sure nothing happens to it (see Genesis 2:15). Adam was to be the keeper and protector of not only the garden, but also of everything that God had given him.

Men, you and I are to be the protectors of our wives, our children, our environment, our communities and our churches. We are to never allow anything that could hinder the delicate, delightful presence of peace and joy in the Holy Ghost from coming into the presence of our homes, our church or our community. We are to protect our families against the onslaught of Internet pornography; abusive music that degrades women and teaches rebellion against authority; against legalized gambling in the form of casinos and even lotteries; and against the growing tide of gang violence and drug abuse. It is only when we, as men, get in and stay in the presence of God—through the person of Jesus Christ—that we can live up to this plan and purpose and find our true identity. As fathers, when we fulfill our God-given plan and work out our God-given purpose, we become the glory of our children.

The glory of children is their father.

> *Children's children are the crown of old men, and the glory of children is their father.*
> —Proverbs 17:6

The Bible says that the glory of the husband is the wife. The children, then, are the glory of the wife, and the glory of the children, then, is the father. The wife makes the husband look good. And the children make the wife look good. Well, then, what makes children look good? Their father. In other words, the radiant reflection of children is their father. He represents all they can be and more. In the father they see their hope fulfilled, their destiny complete and their dreams realized. Fathers act out before their children all of the possibilities that belong to them within the world community.

> *I do not write these things to shame you, but as my beloved children I warn you. For though you might have ten thousand instructors in Christ, yet you do not have many fathers; for in Christ Jesus I have begotten you through the gospel. Therefore I urge you, imitate me.*
> —1 Corinthians 4:14-16

In writing to the church at Corinth, Paul establishes in these few words the connectivity of fathers in everything that is spiritual and meaningful in the world today. Not only must we apply that to our natural fathers, but also to spiritual fathers; therefore, the glory of children is their father. They are more than instructors; they are reflectors of the glory and purpose of Father God.

Imitate me. Another time Paul said, *The things which you learned and received and heard and saw in me, these do...* (Philippians 4:9). In other words, he is saying that I'm going to imitate Christ and you should imitate me. Whatever the father does, even in the home, says to the children, "You follow me and I will show you the way. I am the pathfinder, the pioneer, the discoverer and I am preparing a way for you that is worthy to follow."

My father, George, gave my brothers, Tony, William, Rodney and me something that has had a lasting impact on our lives. He gave us the opportunity to get both religious and academic training by insisting that our mother keep us in parochial schools. Each of us graduated from Purcell High School in Cincinnati, Ohio. Two of us, Tony and I, graduated from Xavier University of Cincinnati, Ohio, and William and Rodney graduated from the University of Cincinnati. We were the first in the family line to attend and graduate from college.

Although they never married, George and my mother, Mamie, worked together to see to it that their sons grew up with an academic as well as a moral foundation. George was primarily a provider of moral support and encouragement. Never a wealthy man...but always a survivor, he has provided me with the determination that has helped me to raise three children, who are all grown now and doing well. They each know and love Jesus Christ and have a solid moral foundation. But most of all, R.J., Ashley and Bradley, our children, have benefited from the legacy of their grandfather, George, because they too have grown up with a foundation of unconditional love. Cynthia and I love those three children with all the love in our hearts.

It was not only George's unconditional love but it was my mother, Mamie's tremendous gift of compassion and mercy that has helped me through the years. I'll talk more about her capacity to care later.

George revealed something that I have now come to understand as the *"spirit of fatherhood."* Even though there were times when the physical presence of fatherhood was missing because of his and Mamie's relationship, the spirit of fatherhood hovered over us continually.

George was our foundation, and because of his and our mother's commitment to us, my brothers and I are each raising our families with a solid foundation of unconditional love and commitment.

FATHER REFLECTIONS

1. *What male figure built a firm foundation in your life? Have you thanked him?*

2. *What steps can you now take to build a similar foundation in the lives of a new generation?*

3. *Who is "imitating you"? Are you proud or ashamed of the example you are setting for the next generation?*

4. *What will be the legacy and the impact that you leave on your children and your children's children?*

CHAPTER THREE

Father—Why Do We Seek to Please Him?

"He is our inspiration."

> *Small boys become big men through the influence of big men who care about small boys.*
> —Anonymous

> *I watched a small man with thick calluses on both hands work fifteen and sixteen hours a day. I saw him once literally bleed from the bottoms of his feet, a man who came here uneducated, alone, unable to speak the language, who taught me all I needed to know about faith and hard work by the simple eloquence of his example.*
> —Mario Cuomo,
> former Governor of New York City

It is important to consider how we all have been conditioned in life by our relationships and our contact with our fathers. Our childhood environment and upbringing determine a great deal about how we see ourselves as we really are. Often the rules and regulations that we grow up with and are placed under by our fathers may be culturally imposed but not necessarily biblically reflective.

Our relationship with our fathers will have a lifelong impact on us and will go a long way in shaping how we learn to feel loved and cared for, to feel secure and safe, to feel important and fulfilled in life. If you lost your father early in life, or if he abandoned you or harmed you, the first major taste of pain and disappointment in life may be traced back to your father.

Regardless of the presence of your father and regardless of whether his presence was loving and nurturing on one hand or abusive and neglectful on the other hand, your father remains a key player and a *force* in the outcome of your life. Your relationship with your father dramatically impacts how you learn to relate to women if you are male and to men if you are female, and his presence contributes to your first impression of God.

Author Stephen Covey said, *"Role modeling is the most basic responsibility of parents. Parents are handing life's scripts to their children, scripts that in all likelihood will be acted out for the rest of the children's lives."* The life of the father deeply impacts the lives of his children, and that impact, whether good or bad, will be replicated in the adult years of the children. It is the father's behavior, more than his words, that writes a script upon a child's life, and that script will be rewritten in the next generation. It is important that fathers write the script correctly the first time.

If fathers fail to take advantage of teachable moments, tender moments and those fleeting moments when their children cry out and seek their comfort, strength, wisdom or knowledge, it could result in a wounded child. Obviously if a man is abusive, negligent or absent from his child's life, that child will potentially be impacted by a father wound for the rest of his or her life.

FATHER WOUNDS

Father wounds are among the most devastating and hardest wounds to heal. Their pain can endure for many years, continuing to impact the actions of the adult child. Because we all have this natural desire to please our fathers and a natural need to have him as a major source of inspiration for us, suffering inflicted by a father has an eternal quality to it. No matter how hard the child tries, the impact of a father wound will continue to fester and foster negative actions and reactions.

Salman Rushdie writes, *"The reality of a father is a weight few sons can bear."* The weight that is hard to bear is the weight of pain inflicted by a father. This pain may be the result of the hurt that flows from a heart that has been inflicted by injurious words or even physical abuse from an angry father. It may be the inheritance of bitterness, disappointment and anger created by a father being absent during the child's earlier years. It may be the weight of a father's pain being inflicted on the next generation. All of these are heavy weights to bear.

A father has *the force*, the natural power, to inspire his children to accomplish great things or to stunt the health and growth of his family. Too often many fathers have a negative relationship with their children marred by verbal and sometimes even physical abuse or by his absence. Instead of being a loving protector and provider who is the encourager and inspiration for his children, a father who does not understand *the force* of fatherhood can easily become his children's cause for shame and lack of self-esteem.

I can never remember a time when George physically spanked, paddled or whipped me. My mother on the other hand…I remember. But I carried a father wound for years, until I realized the blessing that George's decision had been. You see, George insisted that we attend Catholic school, and he worked two and sometimes three jobs to see to it that we did. I hated going to Catholic school. First because we had to wear those silly uniforms, and then because we simply were not like the other guys who went to public school. And it seemed that of the brothers I was the vocal one who expressed my displeasure and dislike of going to Catholic school. George was always patient and calm with me, but firm. He never wavered—even when my brothers and I did not physically live with him for a time, he made sure we stayed in Catholic school.

The wound came one day when I was in the fourth grade and needed new shoes. Well, George being the junk collector that he was got me some "new shoes." They were the most hideous reddish-brown, box-toe shoes you have ever seen. To top it off they were "used." He had found them in the garbage as he made his rounds collecting trash early on Saturday. He made me wear those shoes to school, and I thought I was going to die. Everyone laughed at me, and then the most horrible thing that could happen happened.

St. Paul's school was predominately white, although an inner-city school. The white kids were driven in from the suburbs, while we walked to school. Well, it just so happened that the area of town where George had collected trash and found the shoes was an area where several of the white kids lived. Yep, you guessed it. One of the fifth graders recognized the shoes as the ones his parents had thrown away only days earlier. They had belonged to his grandfather! I don't think I spoke to my dad for about a month. I could not understand why he would be so cruel as to make me wear those shoes to school each day.

I got over it eventually, but it wounded me for a long time. We must remember that since there are no perfect people, more likely than not, somewhere along the way, we will suffer a father wound or some disappointment in our relationship with our fathers.

Without our fathers, we have no real sense of what it means to be special, to be different, to be loved, adored and to be accepted unconditionally. *The force* and power of a loving father, even one who is human and who makes mistakes, cannot be underestimated. Fathers will make mistakes, but it is up to the father to minimize and to correct those mistakes in the life of his child.

"Boys grow into men with a wounded father within, a conflicted sense of masculinity," wrote Samuel Osherson, a Harvard research psychologist. After scores of interviews with men in their thirties and forties, Osherson concluded, *"the psychological or physical absence of fathers from their families is one of the great underestimated tragedies of our times."* [5]

The father wounds that exist in so many people in our society can at least partially be reflected in the decaying nature of the culture around us. These wounds are embedded in our human psyche and prevent children from attaining

---

[5] Samuel Osherson, *Finding Our Fathers* (New York, Fawcett Columbine, 1987) 6.

their ultimate potential. Consider the words you speak and contemplate their influence on your children: *"You're stupid." "You'll never amount to anything." "Why can't you be like your brother?" "You have such great potential." "I believe in you." "I am so proud of you."*

At some point the cycle must be broken, and now is the time for men (and women) to open their hearts to the Great Healer. As their hearts are healed, they will be able to

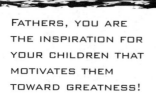

FATHERS, YOU ARE THE INSPIRATION FOR YOUR CHILDREN THAT MOTIVATES THEM TOWARD GREATNESS!

effectively forgive their fathers and then father their own children without inflicting upon them the wounds that they suffered. Then the healing can begin for our nation.

The force of fatherhood has such power in our lives that one way or another we will be impacted and shaped by how he relates to us and we to him. I shall never forget the impact of George making me wear those shoes, but neither will I ever forget the positive impact he had on my life. His spirit of entrepreneurship is indelibly imbedded in my spirit. George always had a job or two, as well as a "side gig," as he would say.

I can remember the other kids in the neighborhood laughing at us each Saturday morning as we had to get up early and get in the dump truck that was used to haul garbage. Although he worked as an auto mechanic at a used car lot, this was one of George's "side gigs." We would get up and go through our neighborhood collecting anything that others threw away. Then we'd head for the suburbs to collect garbage in the white neighborhoods and take it to the landfill.

This is where we could get all our household items—"new" toys, games, footballs, basketballs, baseball equipment, and sometimes even clothes.

Rather than this experience leaving scars, shame or inferiority complexes in my life, it left me with a tremendous work ethic, sense of self-responsibility and a determination to own and operate my own business. In order to please my father, I have carried this work ethic and spirit of entrepreneurship into my life.

It is this spirit of entrepreneurship that God has converted into a passion to plant and grow churches. The first church we officially organized had five people meeting in a small two-bedroom inner-city housing project. The Galilean Baptist Church grew because of the hand of God and the spirit of entrepreneurship that I inherited from my dad. In six years we went from those five members to more than 400 members, serving literally hundreds of thousands of dollars worth of food, clothes, utility assistance, and other aid to the poor and underserved.

In 1988 the burning passion to serve and not be served (and the thought of taking other people's old clothes) caused a divine discontent (the spirit of entrepreneurship) to rise up in me, and we gave birth to the Nations Ford Baptist Church, now Nations Ford Community Church. We left Galilean and started from nothing with seven people in our living room. We had only a dream, a vision, and a determination to not take any more "hand-me-downs." Nations Ford Community Church now has over 3,500 members, has given birth to four daughter congregations and has assisted in starting over twelve other new churches. Think about it! From hauling garbage to reaching out with the helping hand of Christ. From being laughed at because of those ugly reddish-brown shoes to distributing shoes to those in need. What a transition, all because of *the father force.*

A SON WHO PLEASED HIS FATHER

The life of Jesus Christ serves as a wonderful example to us of the need to please our fathers. He did nothing without the motivation of pleasing His Father. This was the major motivation in the life of Jesus, and I believe it is a healthy motivation for our lives when our fathers are walking with God and being the father force in our lives.

> *Then Jesus came from Galilee to the Jordan to John to be baptized by him. But John protested strenuously, having in mind to prevent Him, saying, It is I who have need to be baptized by You, and do You come to me? But Jesus replied to him, Permit it just now; for this is the fitting way for [both of] us to fulfill all righteousness [that is, to perform completely whatever is right]. Then he permitted Him. And when Jesus was baptized, He went up at once out of the water; and behold, the heavens were opened, and he [John] saw the Spirit of God descending like a dove and alighting on Him. And behold, a voice from heaven said, This is My Son, My Beloved, in Whom I delight!*
> —Matthew 3:13-17 AMP

Jesus was so motivated and inspired by His Father that He said on one occasion that He did nothing except what He saw His father do. He also said nothing except what He heard His Father say (see John 5:19).

Just as a father can have a negative impact on his child through the wounds of angry words and negative actions, so also, a father can positively impact a child through encouraging words and positive actions. The *force* of a father's words and actions can never be minimized—it is one of the greatest sources of inspiration in our world.

Many sons and daughters have gone on to live productive and meaningful lives simply because they have always held a picture of their father's approval in their minds.

> *I just owe almost everything to my father [and] it's passionately interesting for me that the things that I learned in a small town, in a very modest home, are just the things that I believe have won the election.*
> —Margaret Thatcher
> Former British prime minister

> *It's only when you grow up, and step back from him, or leave him for your own career and your own home—it's only then that you measure his greatness and fully appreciate it. Pride reinforces love.*
> —Margaret Truman
> Daughter of former president

> *My father taught me that the only way you can make good at anything is to practice, and then practice some more.*
> —Pete Rose
> Former baseball player

I will ever be grateful for the wise counsel of a strong and inspired father when he taught, "If you always say no to the first temptation, you will not have to worry if you will be able to say no to the second one."
—Harold Hillman
Philosopher

My father gave me the greatest gift anyone could give another person, he believed in me.
—Jim Valvano
Former college basketball coach

We all have barriers to overcome and we use the nine values (courage, determination, teamwork, persistence, integrity, citizenship, justice, commitment, and excellence) my father used to get over our barriers.
—Sharon Robinson
Daughter of Jackie Robinson

Fathers inspire us, encourage us, give us direction, help us resolve our problems and provide resources to fulfill our destiny. There is no greater force in the universe than the father force.

FATHERS PROTECT US FROM EVIL

Not only are fathers a source of inspiration for good, they are also a force that keeps us from evil. I recall the story of a dear friend, a lovely lady, and I am sure she was a stunningly attractive young girl when she was in her teens and early twenties. She tells of going to a party during her freshman year of college. Sometime during the night she decided she needed to leave the party because she was simply not enjoying it. When asked why, she replied, "Someone started smoking some marijuana and there was drinking going on. And even though I wanted to be there and take part, in my mind, I kept thinking, what would happen if my daddy walked through that door?"

THE UNIVERSAL AND ETERNAL FORCE OF A FATHER

Many fathers who are not aware of the power of fatherhood have made the mistake of abusing their power and misusing their leadership role and their influence. Instead of inspiring, covering, protecting and providing for their children, because of their own weaknesses, they end up manipulating and unreasonably controlling their sons and daughters.

When sons and daughters have positive encouragement and inspiration from their fathers, they grow up well balanced and able to face life's difficulties without the pressure of trying to be perfect. They grow up knowing they are unique, different, special and capable of adding value to any situation in which they find themselves. They are inspired to greatness because they are motivated out of love to please their father.

WHEN A FATHER UNDERSTANDS THE FORCE OF FATHERHOOD, HE WILL USE HIS POWER TO INSPIRE HIS CHILDREN TO GREATNESS AND TO THE FULFILLMENT OF THEIR DIVINE DESTINY.

A father has the power to give his children roots and wings—roots that will stabilize and anchor their lives in God, and wings that will give them the courage to fly away from home to discover their own destiny. Fathers are the fertilizer for the soil and the wind beneath their wings. They nourish and encourage. They send and lead. They comfort and correct. They compel and propel.

Children both admire and fear their father's strength. On one hand they want their father to be strong and powerful (in the sense of being self-confident and determined), but they may also be frightened at times by that power. Walking the middle ground between dominance and permissiveness can sometimes be difficult for a father. It is this ability to travel between these two realms that increases the father's influence in their lives. A balance between exercising authority and granting freedom gives children security and confidence.

The father exercises great influence in the psychological development of his children. In order to effectively increase his influence, it is important that the father spend qualitative time getting to know them—their fears, aspirations, abilities and struggles. As the father gets to know his children he will be able to more competently direct them in the ways of the Lord.

LOVE—THE MOST POWERFUL INFLUENCE

> *"For the Father loveth the Son, and sheweth him all things that himself doeth..."*
> —John 5:20 KJV

There is no greater force in the world than the love of a father for his son or daughter. When children feel accepted and respected by their father, they will begin to develop close feelings of mutual affection. Fathers who are never involved with their children and are either too permissive or too dominant are not likely to become close to their children. Fathers who expect to be constantly vigilant disciplinarians, who show no tenderness, create a climate of coldness that puts distance in their relationships. Sometimes the effect can be painful.

By expressing affection through words and deeds, parents send another clear and emphatic message to their children: "I want to be close to you." "I love you." "You are special to me." "I am willing to share myself so you can get to know me better." "You give me joy."

In our closest relationships we seek these bonds of affection. Talking about these feelings has traditionally been easier for women than for men, but a good father must know how to express his love for his child. It is the power of a father's love that will provide an eternal foundation for his children.

A Father Is:

There in every memory
See his love and care
Strength and hands to count on
Freely he does share
Provider, toil so faithfully
To make our dreams come true
Give strong and tender discipline
Though it is hard to do
A Father is God's chosen one
To lead the family
And point it to His will for life
Of love and harmony...

—*Sue Skeen*

FATHER REFLECTIONS

1. *In what ways has your biological or spiritual father propelled and motivated you toward achievement or greatness?*

2. *What "father wounds" have festered in your life? How has the love of the heavenly Father inspired you to heal those wounds?*

3. *What motivates you to please God?*

4. *How would you say that men in our day abuse their power? How does the relationship between the Father and the Son provide an example of balance of power?*

CHAPTER FOUR

Father—What Do We Need Most from Him?

"He is our authority and our protection."

Spiritual warfare involves each and every human being, especially those who have confessed Jesus Christ as Savior and Lord of their lives. Satan knows that if he can undermine and cause division in the home, between husband and wife and between fathers and their children, he undercuts God's plan to reveal His love in the one institution that best reflects His plan and purpose—the family.

Therefore, as fathers we must understand how we are going to be attacked and how our family, community, church and culture will be attacked and how to respond to those satanic influences. Fathers have a tremendous responsibility for their families—far greater than I first realized when I got married over thirty years ago. But the more I studied the Scriptures the more I realized how much the Word of God reveals the responsibilities of fathers.

One of the major responsibilities that grabbed my attention was the father's responsibility to protect his wife and children, and even his environment. A father who understands fatherhood knows that whatever he allows to come into his home will either have a positive or negative effect on his wife and children. As fathers we must be very sensitive to this so that the environment of our home is conducive to raising children who love God and who desire to follow Him.

A SATANIC STRATEGY AGAINST FATHERS

Since the father is so vital to the spiritual life of the family, where do you think Satan is going to attack in order to get the family off course? He is going to attack the father so that he can get to the children and to his wife. The father will not be able to resist these forces by willpower alone. This battle is of a spiritual nature and can only be won with spiritual power.

> *...human will-power alone is not enough. Will-power is excellent and we should always be using it; but it is not enough. A desire to live a good life is not enough. Obviously we should all have that desire, but it will not guarantee success. So let me put it thus: Hold on to your principles of morality and ethics, use your willpower to the limit, pay great heed to every noble, uplifting desire that is in you; but realize that these things alone are not enough, that they will never bring you to the desired place. We have to realize that all our best is totally inadequate, that a spiritual battle must be fought in a spiritual manner.*
> —Dr. D. Martyn Lloyd-Jones,
> noted pastor and author in Wales

For fathers to rise to their greatest potential they must understand that there is another world that is not seen—a world of the spirit. In that world there are great forces that we cannot see. These forces are either contributing to the fulfillment of Father's plan in this world or they are working against that plan. The evil side of these forces must be understood and fought against. Where does a man get this information in such a secular world that does not believe in this other world? He must turn to Father. The Scriptures give us great insight into how that can be done.

> *"When the strong man, fully armed, [from his courtyard] guards his own dwelling, his belongings [goods] are undisturbed [his property is at peace and is secure]. But when one stronger than he attacks him and conquers him, he robs him of his whole armor on which he had relied and divides up and distributes all his goods as plunder (spoil)."*
>
> Luke 11:21-22 AMP

Jesus said in Mark 3:27, *"No man can enter into a strong man's house, and spoil his goods, except he first binds the strong man"* (paraphrase mine). We can apply this verse to how Satan attacks the family. In order for Satan to come into and destroy a father's goods (his wife, his children and their environment) or his home, Satan has to attack and bind the father, the strong man, and then go after his family. The word goods can refer to the children, the wife and all that they are supposed to become in the sight of God. If Satan can keep the father from fulfilling his role, and if he can restrain the father from protecting his family, he will gain access to the whole family. This satanic strategy is the cause for the great breakdown in the American culture and has contributed to the deterioration of the father force in American society.

The battle to maintain a father's goods (his wife, his children, his home, health, business or career) begins with him, as a man, understanding his God-given power and authority. When men understand that God has a divine purpose for their lives and that they have been divinely equipped with the force of fatherhood, we will see a tremendous impact and transformation of our culture.

Discovering the power of God

A Christian father has the force of God—the power and the authority through the name of Jesus Christ—to protect his wife and family physically, socially, and spiritually. The force that makes a father strong is not to be found in this world. It comes from a higher power, a heavenly power. This power gives him the ability to physically stand between his family and any possible physical harm. Socially, he is able to absorb the pressures of situations that may be awkward or compromising and not allow his family to go unprotected. Spiritually, a father has been given the power to stand between his family and the powers of darkness in this world and the rulers of spiritual wickedness in heavenly places.

In order to tap into this power, a father must develop a deeper and more intimate relationship with God. It is not enough to have a surface relationship with God. In order to survive this satanic attack against him he must be willing to go deeper. He must learn to open his spirit and soul to God. As he spends more time in the presence of God he will discover a new source of power and authority flowing into his spirit that will then empower his soul. His spiritual relationship with God is critical to his being able to stand against the evil one. Happy is the one who walks so close to God that he leaves no room for the devil to slip between.

Through his relationship with God as Father, a man can discover new abilities and new gifts to fulfill the father's role as priest and protector in his home. There will be times when he will not have the wisdom or the power to protect his family. His resources are discovered in the presence of God. As he lives in His presence he will discover the authority to stand for his family against any attack of the enemy.

THE AUTHORITY OF THE FATHER

Standing in the strength of his heavenly Father, a man will be able to force the devil to recognize his authority in his home. A father who is surrendered to the lordship of Jesus Christ will, by his very presence, create a protective environment in the home. The authority of this unseen spiritual protection—emotionally, mentally, materially, spiritually, or otherwise—will repel anything that is not the will of God.

A father protects that which is true. If he is going to protect what is true, he must know what is true. This will require spiritual discernment, a discernment that is only possible as he opens himself to the voice of God. In protection of the truth, a father who understands fatherhood will stand against that which is not true when it attempts to invade his home through music, through the Internet or through other sources of modern technology. He will combat the lies of the culture as it seeks to encroach on the lives of his family. His spiritual antenna is always up and functioning, detecting any lie that seeks to enter his home. He is the ultimate truth detector.

A father who understands the force of fatherhood will exercise his authority to bind and to loose. A father who understands the force of fatherhood will protect his son and daughter from mental attitudes that cause serious emotional traumas later on in life. Spiritual discernment with spiritual wisdom will create a pathway that will lead his family to all truth, protecting them from the subtleties of the enemy.

FATHERS—THE SOURCE OF TRUE PROTECTION

True protection deals with shielding the family, protecting the community, protecting the church and protecting the nations against the onslaught of Satan. It means protecting our moral environment against the pollution of pornography, the abomination of abortion and the cancer of cultural relativism. Fathers must step up and protect their culture from the escalation of violence and rampant abuse.

I am concerned that unless fathers use their God-given spiritual authority to resist and cast down the evil tidal wave of Internet pornography, we will see more child abductions, molestations and abuse than history can record over the next ten years. Fathers are like God's ultimate security guards for our society. When the father shows up, everyone in the family, the community or the church is supposed to feel protected and secure.

Earlier I mentioned that my wife and I have three children. Our daughter is the middle child and we have a son one year younger. When Ashley and Bradley went off to college and we experienced the "empty nest," it was not long before

I got a call from both of them. Ashley was concerned and a bit confused about the newly found freedom of college life, and she did not feel comfortable about being there. When she called I assured her, *"Sweetheart, you are going to do fine; I have confidence in you and I am sure that you will be all right."* It was not long before Bradley called. He was homesick and he felt as if his life was falling apart. But when he heard the voice of his father saying, *"Son, it's going to be okay, and you are going to do fine; I have every bit of confidence in you,"* suddenly everything fell into place. Why? Because their father spoke reassuring words of confidence, protecting their emotions and protecting their self-esteem.

Taking care of your family

Fathers are designed and commanded to fight against sin and Satan and everything he uses to attack the family and the cultural environment in which our children must grow and our wives must live. The Bible tells us that God took the man [father] and put him in the garden of Eden to take care of it (see Genesis 2:15). Fathers were designed to "take care of"—to guard and to protect—the garden and everything in it. That includes the plants, the animals, even the woman who would be created to live in the garden with the man. God did not tell the woman to protect anything. Why not? The reason is because the woman is one of the created beings that the man [father] is supposed to protect.

God commanded the man [father] to protect everything that is in his care and under his authority, so the father is a natural protector. He is built to protect in every way, physically, mentally and emotionally.

A father who understands the force of fatherhood will do everything within his power to exercise his God-given authority over the forces of the darkness and to protect everything that God has placed under his sphere of responsibility. Yes, a father has an awesome responsibility to be the professor of that which is good; the producer to replenish the earth; the provider of esteem and identity; but one of the major roles of the father is that of a protector.

THE FATHER IS THE PRIMARY PROTECTOR OF HIS FAMILY AND ENVIRONMENT

As mentioned previously, God asked Adam what was going on when Satan tempted and deceived Eve, because Adam was God's appointed protector. It was his job to see that the garden was safe from harm and danger of any kind. As security guard of the garden, he was to protect it against all attacks. God specifically put Adam in charge in order to take care of things and to ensure that nothing went wrong. In order for a father to effectively care for and protect his family, he must develop a warrior's spirit.

DEVELOPING A WARRIOR SPIRIT

The war is real, therefore either gird up your loins and fight or have your destiny, your future, your hope and your blessings taken from you, by your enemy.

For fathers, there is no place for timidity and passivity on any battlefield—and the family is on the battlefield. There are forces of evil that are seeking to destroy you and your family. War is vicious, vigorous, aggressive and overwhelming. War is an all-out encounter with the enemy. War is not just waiting around in a defensive posture hoping that the enemy does not bring the battle to you. No, spiritual warfare is you, as the *father force*, taking the battle to the enemy. War is offensive!

The natural tendency is for all of us to hit the ground when the arrows of lies, the rocks of rejection, the bombs of sickness, the shells of sin, and the darts of deception and distrust are flying over our heads. When the enemy attacks we tend to retreat, to duck and to hit the ground looking for cover. It isn't wrong to hit the ground for a little bit. The harsh realities of living in a world of evil will stun and stump even the strongest. But a true father will rise up and stand to protect himself and his family from any satanic attack.

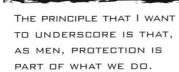

THE PRINCIPLE THAT I WANT TO UNDERSCORE IS THAT, AS MEN, PROTECTION IS PART OF WHAT WE DO. WE OUGHT TO BE WILLING TO RISK ALL THAT WE HAVE, INCLUDING OUR OWN LIVES IF NECESSARY, TO PROTECT OUR FAMILIES...

Any good soldier knows that the longer he just lies there, the greater the likelihood is that he will become a casualty of the war. If he just goes home and sits in a corner, turns out the lights and pouts, or gets in the bed and mopes and complains and whines and cries and has a pity-party, hoping that the nightmare of the battle will go away, he will be destroyed. Sooner or later a soldier must get up and fight off the attacking forces of the enemy—or die!

Jesus did not come to earth, die on the cross of Calvary, give you all His authority, power, gifts, wisdom, strength and the power to use His Name in an unlimited manner so you could run from the enemy. He didn't shed His precious blood, defeat death, hell and the grave, rise from the dead, ascend into heaven, make an open show of Satan and render his power null and void and sit down at the right hand of the Father to be your intercessor and your mediator of every good gift just so you could sit around and be intimidated, frustrated, discouraged and defeated as a child of God! He did all of this so that you could enter into His victory.

The Bible says of Jesus, *The Son of God appeared for this purpose, that He might destroy the works of the devil* (1 John 3:8 NASB).

God is saying that you need to have a warrior spirit. God wants you to thrive—to live in abundance, prosperity and health—so you can be a blessing to your family. But if you shrink back in the day of battle you will never make it; you will miss out and your family will suffer.

So many great men of God in the Scriptures had the spirit of a warrior: Abraham, Moses, Joshua, Caleb, David, Peter, Paul and so many, many more. The warrior spirit is a shielding, defending, guarding, protecting attitude. It is a spirit of disciplined, assertive and sometimes aggressive action. It is the warrior spirit that will protect your family at all costs.

A saint with a warrior spirit will not turn and run from a just cause. Those with a warrior spirit will never run from the devil and his schemes, and whenever he raises the stakes, those with a warrior spirit will call his bluff and raise him again! In today's society we are in an all-out war, and it will take men with warrior spirits to protect their families from the destructive forces that are impinging upon their territory.

A man with a warrior spirit is one who is willing to step out of his comfort zone to stand in the gap for the sake of his family. He will do whatever it takes to prepare himself physically and spiritually for war.

Warriors dress for battle every day

A believer with a warrior spirit will dress daily with the whole armor of God. He knows how to put on the girdle of truth, the breastplate of righteousness, the shoes of the gospel of peace, the helmet of salvation, the shield of faith and the sword of the Spirit, which is the Word of God (see Ephesians 6:11-17).

Satan is not going to fight against you when you are not a threat to his influence in your family. A warrior puts on the whole armor every day! When you put on and use the whole protective equipment and armor given to you by the Father, you are totally protected from the crown of your head to the soles of your feet—except for one area—your back.

Never turn your back on your enemy!

This is significant and it has a twofold meaning. First, it means that you should never, ever turn your back on the devil. If you do, you are giving him an opportunity to wound you in an unprotected area. Never turn around. Never walk away and say, "I've had enough." Never turn around and say, "I can't stand this anymore. I can't take anymore." Success is a ladder you cannot climb with your hands in your pockets while turning your back to the enemy. It takes the power of will and determination to resist the enemy face on. Gandhi said that strength does not come from physical capability but from an indomitable will. Dr. Martin Luther King, Jr. put it this way, "Our lives begin to end the day we become silent about things that matter." You resist turning your back through facing your problems head on with a courageous determination. When the battle gets tough, always remember that you are not in the war by yourself.

GOD'S GOT YOUR BACK!

The good news is that you are not in this battle alone. God is just as concerned about the protection of your family as you are. The "God who is there" is always there to protect and strengthen you so you can protect and strengthen your family. You are not alone. There is One who is there for you.

> *He has not made us for naught; He has brought us thus far, in order to bring us further, in order to bring us on to the end. He will never leave us nor forsake us; so that we may boldly say, "The Lord is my Helper; I will not fear what flesh can do unto me." We "may cast all our care upon Him who careth for us." What is it to us how our future path lies, if it be but His path? What is it to us whither it leads us, so that in the end it leads to Him? What is it to us what He puts upon us, so that He enables us to undergo it with a pure conscience, a true heart, not desiring anything of this world in comparison of Him? What is it to us what terror befalls us, if He be but a hand to protect and strengthen us?*
> —John Henry Cardinal Newman
> (1801-1889, England)

Fathers, you and I are to be the protector of our wives, our children, our environment, our communities and our churches. We are to never allow anything that could keep the delicate, delightful presence of peace and joy in the Holy Ghost from coming into our homes, our churches or our communities.

LIVING IN THE VICTORIOUS FEAR OF THE LORD

We are living in a culture that has lost all fear of God! Some are calling this the "No Fear" generation. "No Fear." Those words seem to be tattooed across the face of our day and time. That speaks volumes about the current philosophy of our day. Certainly, it is a positive thing to be free from the paralyzing pain of fear. No father can effectively fulfill his role in the family if he is frozen by fear. Fear can keep him from being able to make decisions and act on behalf of his family. But there is a freedom from fear that is not appropriate—no fear of authority, no fear of consequences, and ultimately, no fear of God. There is a fear for fathers that is healthy—the fear of the Lord. It is this fear of the Lord that will guide him in protecting his family.

What does it mean to "fear God?" It is not living with the idea that God has a big stick or big hammer and that He is just waiting to smash you over the head at the least little thing you might do wrong! I am not talking about being *afraid* of being in the presence of God or coming to God. As a loving, merciful Father, God calls us to …*come boldly to the throne of grace, that we may obtain mercy and find grace to help in time of need* (Hebrews 4:16). Not only that, but as your loving and gracious heavenly Father, God wants you to come to Him and be in His presence because in His presence is the fullness of your joy (see Psalm 16:11).

So then the fear of the Lord is not hiding from a brutal, mean, angry or abusive father. On the contrary, the fear of the Lord is having a conscious awareness that God is watching and that you can approach Him. However, this is where multitudes have missed it and where many in today's performances called "revivals" have led countless people astray. There are those who teach people to approach God as though He was just "one of the boys," or as if He is "a man like we are." There are those who do not fear God and thus have taught others that when you are in the presence of God you act silly and bark like dogs or make noises like animals. That is totally preposterous and not biblical. It shows disrespect for the dignity of a holy God who does all things well and decently and in order.

The fear of the Lord *means living in such a manner that you want to do nothing to displease or disappoint God! Why? It is because you respect Him so much and because you are so thankful and grateful for His love, His mercy, His grace, His peace, His joy, His provision, and His protection.*

The fear of the Lord *is a wholesome fear of displeasing a loving Father. It is the thought of bowing down to and before God in awe and wonder, in respect for who He is, the awesome creator of the universe who is in total and complete control.*

The fear of the Lord *is a healthy concept for the believer because it is not simply an intellectual acknowledgment of God…it is a willful, daily surrender to Him and His will.*

To fear the Lord *means to stand in awe, to reverence, to honor, to have a healthy respect for the Lord God because you recognize Him as worthy of the utmost esteem and desire to please Him only.*

THE FEAR OF THE LORD IS STRENGTH FOR FATHERS

Walking in the fear of the Lord will help fathers gain strength to protect their families. It is a powerful motivation that supports and strengthens you, as a father, to take seriously the responsibility that God has given you to protect your family.

The Scriptures clearly show us that you and I are commanded to fear God. It is not a divine suggestion nor is it a multiple-choice question. The Bible commands that God's people live in "fear of the Lord." Deuteronomy 10:12 says, *"And now, Israel, what does the Lord your God require of you, but to fear the Lord your God, to walk in all His ways and to love Him, to serve the Lord your God with all your heart and with all your soul"* (emphasis added).

> A FATHER'S DESIRE TO PLEASE AND RESPECT AND HONOR THE HEAVENLY FATHER WILL GIVE HIM THE MOTIVATION AND COURAGE TO WATCH OVER HIS OWN FAMILY.

Ecclesiastes 12:13 says, *Let us hear the conclusion of the whole matter: Fear God and keep His commandments, for this is man's all.* Jesus said, *"And do not fear those who kill the body but cannot kill the soul. But rather fear Him who is able to destroy both soul and body in hell"* (Matthew 10:28). Peter writes to the church in 1 Peter 2:17, *Honor all people. Love the brotherhood. Fear God. Honor the king.*

The fear of the Lord will build character into your life and support you in your responsibility for your family. As the fear of the Lord becomes your primary motivation, you will discover the spiritual compensations that will come to you and your family.

THE COMPENSATION FOR THE MAN WHO FEARS THE LORD

God is gracious and full of compassion. He is long-suffering toward us, and *His mercies are new every morning, His compassion fails not and great is His faithfulness* (see Lamentations 3:22-23). And it is because of His grace, His mercy, and His long-suffering toward us that God has chosen to compensate or reward those who live in the fear of Him. God is not compelled to give us anything. He does not have to move on our behalf or show us kindness. However, because He is a covenant-keeping God who loves you and your family with an unconditional love, He will reward all those who live in reverence, awe, honor, and respect of Him and His Word.

Psalm 112:1 declares, *Blessed is the man who fears the Lord...* and in verses 7-8 the Scriptures declare, *He will not be afraid....* Fathers, when you fear the Lord you need not fear anything else. The fear of the Lord God is the fear that conquers fear. Notice what blessings and benefits there are to the family when the father, the man of the house, "walks in the fear of the Lord." Verse one says he is *"blessed who fears the Lord."* There is happiness or contentment for the man who fears the Lord. Whatever other men think of them or say about them, God says that the father who fears Him will be blessed; and His saying so makes it so!

In this chapter we see four blessings that come to the father who fears the Lord. These blessings will be transferred to his family to the third and fourth generations:

1. When a father fears the Lord, his children will be powerful.

The posterity of a father who fears the Lord will fare well because of his reverence, respect, honor, and the esteem he has for God. *His seed shall be mighty upon earth...* (Psalm 112:2 KVJ). Notice, "His seed" or "descendants" shall be mighty on the earth. Perhaps he himself will not be so great in the world; maybe he himself will not make the cover of *TIME Magazine*, *Newsweek*, or even the local nightly news, but his seed, his sons and his daughters after him, shall be mighty and accomplish much for the glory of the heavenly Father. Too many fathers are spending too much of their valuable time trying to make a name for themselves and robbing their children of the one thing that they can never repay—time. They have no time to invest in their children so that the children can develop a healthy fear of God and grow up to be mighty. The word mighty means that their children will not grow up being weak, lacking faith, knowing little if anything about the grace of God. It means that they will not grow up and fall by the wayside or live godless lives. The word *mighty* in this sense means that they will be godly warriors. The literal meaning is powerful, and the implication is that the children of fathers who fear the Lord God will be warriors, champions or chiefs, who excel and are strong and valiant. Warrior fathers will bring forth warrior children.

Martin Luther King, Sr. was a man who "feared the Lord." His son, and now his son's sons and daughters are becoming "mighty" on the earth. Even when a man who fears the Lord dies and goes to heaven, his legacy will be considerable because his children will walk in his example. Psalm 112:2 continues, ...*the generation of the upright will be blessed*—that is, if they walk in the steps of their fathers who fear the Lord. A man who fears the Lord will protect and establish future generations.

2. When a father fears the Lord, his family will be prosperous.

To the father who will "fear the Lord," the Scriptures promise that his family, his household, shall prosper both materially and spiritually. They shall be blessed with outward prosperity, not according to everything they want, but according to what they need to be a blessing to others. A man who fears the Lord will protect his family from poverty and need.

Wealth and riches shall be in the house of the father who fears the Lord (see Psalm 112:3). Wealth and riches will be in your "house," that is, in your family heritage. A man who fears the Lord will receive blessings from the Lord and will be able to pass on those blessings to his children, thus, securing their future.

But notice something much better: the verse also says, *his righteousness shall last forever.* His family will be blessed with spiritual blessings, which are the true riches. The wealth and prosperity of the father who fears the Lord will be in his house, and some day those riches will be passed on to his children. It has been said, *Grace is better than gold, because when your gold is gone, grace will live on.* The father who fears and reverences God is one who can handle wealth and riches. He can be trusted with wealth and riches, and still keep his reverence, awe, and honor of the Lord God.

Worldly prosperity is a blessing only when it does not cause you to lose your "fear of God." When a true father can bless his family with wealth and riches and still persevere in the fruit of the Spirit: love, joy, peace, long-suffering, kindness, goodness, faithfulness, gentleness, and self-control (see Galatians 5:22-23), that family is blessed indeed.

3. When a father fears the Lord, his family will be protected.

When a family faces darkness, afflictions, difficulties and tough times, the father who fears the Lord, will not bail out or ignore his troubles. Instead, he will bring "light" or comfort to his family in their hour of affliction. God's promises do not exempt the family from affliction just because the father fears the Lord. Your family will have its share of the common calamities of life, but the good news is that when they come your way, because your family walks in the fear of the Lord, the Lord Himself shall not only bring you light, He will *be* your light. What better way to protect your family!

Anytime a family faces a crisis, whether it is a health, career, relationship or financial crisis, it is difficult to survive, let alone thrive. However, one of the reasons why so many families never recover from crisis is because within the family structure there is something missing—the father force—the power and ability of the father to stand in the gap for his family in times of crisis and face the foes that seek to destroy the fabric of the family. When a father does not fear the

Lord, in times of tribulation he will have no faith in the Lord to bring himself and his family out into victory. Many of those fathers, in the time of crisis, abandon their families. But the man who fears the Lord teaches his family how to release faith in the tough times, encouraging them to ...*walk by faith, not by sight* (2 Corinthians 5:7). He teaches them to trust the Lord who will watch over them. God will protect and keep those who fear Him, and He will give them long life because they reverence His Name!

4. When a father fears the Lord, his decisions will be prudent.

When fathers walk in the fear of the Lord they will have godly wisdom for the management of all their affairs and concerns. When you fear the Lord, you will increase your goods and bless your family with wise and prudent decisions and not have to rely on miracles. You will guide or handle your business affairs with discretion, honor and integrity as God instructs and teaches you.

Fathers who do not fear the Lord will make selfish decisions, which hurt rather than help their families. They will not take into consideration all the implications of their decisions. They will refuse to listen to the counsel of their wives and ultimately make choices for their families that cause hurt, pain and unnecessary hardships.

However, it is part of the character of a man who fears the Lord to use godly wisdom (see James 1:5) so that he can have confidence in managing his affairs. The father who fears the Lord will walk in the spirit of understanding and knowledge and will have the ability to make money legitimately. He will walk in the favor of God and be the lender and not the borrower.

When he speaks, it will be with the wisdom of God. The original Hebrew text reads like this, *He will guide his words with judgment* (see Psalm 112:5). A father who fears the Lord not only will guide his business affairs and family decisions with discretion, but he will also guide his words with judgment. He will use discernment in what he shares in the presence of his family. He will not say any and everything in the presence of his children. He will speak life and not death, blessing and not cursing into their lives.

These are the kinds of fathers we need in our communities and churches today—men who have warrior spirits and know how to walk in the fear of the Lord. They are the fathers who will effectively and consistently protect their families in these changing times. Even more so, they are the fathers who will rise up and enforce the kingdom principles of Scripture. They are the fathers who will be recognized as the father force.

FATHER REFLECTIONS

1. *How does the world distract fathers from fearing the Lord?*

2. *Why do some fathers forfeit their authority in the home? How can a relationship with Christ provide a man with boldness?*

3. *How determined are you to protect your goods? How can you help another father who may be struggling in this area?*

4. *What blessings are being passed down into your family? Which blessings haven't you received? How will your "fear of the Lord" help you to receive those blessings?*

CHAPTER FIVE

Father—Why Does He Give Us What We Need to Have?

"He is our provider."

Something interesting happened when God placed man in the garden to tend and keep it. God first gave man a little bit of Himself as He breathed into man. As His Spirit was breathed into that lifeless body held in the hands of this loving Maker, man became a living being. God then gave man a place to live. He provided a place where His plan could be worked out. God then gave man an assignment, a task, a job and a purpose—to tend, to keep and to rule. God commanded the man to have dominion and to subdue the earth (see Genesis 1:28).

God did not intend for man to leave the garden, being shut out from His precious presence and the constant companionship with his Maker. God commanded the man to take the beauty of life in this garden with all of its splendor and majesty, and to spread this cherished life into the rest of the earth. In essence, we see that God was giving man a command to be a provider for the entire earth. Being a provider is linked to being a protector. A father protects his family by the things he provides for his family.

This divine strategy was all laid out before God gave man the woman. Fathers, God commands you to work and to provide for your families. If you are physically able and not incapacitated or physically handicapped, God expects and your wife and children deserve for you to be the primary source of provision, both materially and spiritually in the home. Fathers are to be productive providers through the means of God-honoring labor.

In my booklet entitled **The Seven Undeniable Principles for Productive Living**, I talk about the need to be productive people because we were created in the image and after the likeness of God. The first thing we see God doing when we are introduced to Genesis 1:1 is being productive. God is creating the heavens and the earth and replenishing them with His image and His likeness. God, who is a creator, created man to be a creator as well. There is a certain imagination, wisdom and ability that is inherent in man that enables him to fulfill this God-given responsibility. Work can be transformed from a curse to a blessing as we embrace the grace to fulfill our role in God's world.

CONNECTING OUR WORK TO OUR HOME

Work was given to fathers for three primary reasons. First, through his work, man is able to advance the plan and purposes of God in expanding His kingdom in the earth. When we engage in commerce and business with ethical and moral standards, we literally extend the kingdom of God into the workplace. By dealing with complex business situations or simple day-to-day tasks using our spiritual gifts and God-given talent, we manifest the life of God.

Secondly, man fills his sense of worth and value when he is engaged in God-honoring work. The Bible says that there is profit in all labor. Each man is created for a unique purpose and is given special gifts in order to fulfill that purpose. No man is totally content until he is filling the void to work. There is a synergy between the fulfillment of his destiny and providing for his family.

Thirdly, man is able to provide for his own household through his work. As man is fulfilling Father's purposes in his life, he is also creating wealth that will provide for all of the needs of his family. There is a holy connectedness between his labor away from home and his provisions for his home. It is a plan that was beautifully worked out in the mind of the Maker.

It is important to understand the order of things. God gave man work and the command to provide before He gave him a woman. Before a man needs a woman, he needs work in order to be a productive provider for the woman whom he will choose. God never commanded the woman to work, even after the fall. God gave the man, not the woman, the responsibility for being the provider of the family.

PROVIDING FOR THE PHYSICAL, SPIRITUAL AND EMOTIONAL NEEDS OF THE FAMILY

As providers, all fathers have three major areas for which they must provide: *physical, spiritual and emotional.* These are the physical necessities of life. The apostle Paul declared that if a man does not work—he should not be allowed to eat (see 2 Thessalonians 3:10), and if a man does not provide for his own household, he is worse than an infidel [unbeliever who is lost in sin] and he has denied the faith (see 1 Timothy 5:8).

All three of these areas must be held in perfect balance. It is not enough to simply be consumed with making money so that we can take care of the physical needs of our families, although providing physically and materially for them is very important. As we fulfill their physical needs we are creating an atmosphere of security for the whole family. A father must be aware of and sensitive to the physical needs of his family, so that through his work, he can provide for and supply those needs. This is especially true when a man has a daughter. She will have more unique and specific needs that boys just don't have.

Between our two sons, R.J. our firstborn and Bradley, there is my little princess or "pumpkin," Ashley. A daughter changes the entire dynamic of what it means to be a provider. And now that Ashley is married with a daughter of her own, I have become a grandfather to little Jada. I have the responsibility of leaving an inheritance not only to my children, but to my children's children. And what a joy that is! Fathers should be actively laying up treasures, not only for the present, but also for the future needs of the family.

Our concern for providing for the physical needs of the family must be balanced with providing for their spiritual needs. We must preserve our energy so that as the father and priest of the house, we can also be spiritually sensitive in order to provide for the spiritual needs of the family. We must create a spiritual atmosphere in the home so the whole family is able to experience the presence of God in powerful and meaningful ways.

In order to fulfill our priestly and prophetic roles in the home, we must be actively developing our own spiritual lives. Fathers should be providing spiritual direction for their families and establishing a moral and ethical value system that will serve as the foundation for the next generation. Fathers are both priests and prophets in the home, and as such, fathers are responsible for the spiritual climate of the house.

At the same time, we must be aware of the family's emotional needs. How do we do that? We provide for the emotional needs of our families by being there when they need us. Often men allow their work outside the home to interfere with providing for their family within the home. It is not uncommon for men to be so tired from their work that when they get home they become absent from their family. This absence creates emotional insecurity in the hearts of children, because the way a father spells love to a child is "T-I-M-E." Our children want their fathers to be there for them, to provide our presence for them—to listen to them, to play with them, and to talk with them. Our love for them is demonstrated more in our actions than in our words. It is certainly important to constantly reassure them of our love with our words, but that love must also be expressed in our involvement in their lives.

A CHRISTMAS I WILL NEVER FORGET

George, my dad, could not provide the finest of things, but he provided the best that he could. I shall always remember that Christmas when I had been begging for a new bike. All the other kids on 12th Street had nice, shining bikes with all the trimmings. My brothers and I shared a bike. I wanted a new bike so badly that it was all I could think of.

Twelfth Street had a steep incline at the end where it intersected with Pendleton Street. A four-way stop sign was there to control traffic, and we loved to get up a head of speed and literally fly down the hill full speed ahead, straight through the intersection, and stop at the corner store. I could see myself doing this on my new bike.

George wouldn't promise me a new bike. He simply said, "I'll see what I can do." That Christmas Eve, after attending midnight mass, I could hardly sleep. Eventually I dozed off. In the morning, when I looked at the bike George had bought for me, I began to cry, then I stomped and ranted and said with tears of disappointment, *"I don't want that bike and I ain't gonna ride it."*

It wasn't the new, shining bike that I had imagined and envisioned. Instead, it looked like George had gone on one of his garbage hunts, found a thrown away bike, repaired it, painted it red and presented it to me. I was crushed. But my harsh words never fazed George outwardly. However, I could see immediately that I had hurt him inwardly. That old, used red Huffy was the best he could do, and he gave it to me with pride.

After a few days of refusing to ride the bike, George looked at me and said, *"Phillip, that is the best I can do, son."* Needless to say, I got on that bike and rode it with pride and joy. That is, until the day I dared to take the 12th Street hill. Rather than flying full speed ahead through the intersection, I turned to see who was watching me so that I could show off. George and my brothers and some others were watching. But when I looked back around, I found myself tangled around the stop sign pole and half of my bike going through the intersection.

I learned from my dad that fathers provide much more than material things; they provide care and compassion, and lessons on how to be grateful and appreciative of the efforts of others. Fathers can create lessons out of most everything that happens in our lives, and George certainly taught me much during that memorable Christmas.

PROVIDING AN IDENTITY FOR YOUR FAMILY

It is obvious that in the natural order the father is to provide food, clothing and shelter for his family. However, the task of provider, as we have shown, goes much farther than providing for the basic physical and material necessities of life.

Fathers are to provide stability, security and a sense of identity for the family. When the father and mother stood at the marriage altar, they became *"Mr. and Mrs."* She took his name. Just as Adam named the woman, *Eve*, when a man and woman marry today, he [the husband] literally names her [the wife]. She leaves the name of her birth and takes the name of his birth. What an awesome responsibility the man now has! The children will have his name. He will be the source of family identity. He can bring them up to the level of his name, or he can take them down to the level of his name.

Fathers, you cannot escape it; whether you are in the home or not, you are responsible for the identity of your offspring, and you provide them with a sense of self-esteem. It may be good or it may be bad, but your name is the source of identity for your family, and you cannot avoid it.

The identity you provide is the character you are building in their lives by your direct interaction with them. As a father you must be prepared to take advantage of everything that happens in their lives. You must be ready to use every situation to create life lessons. Those life lessons will affect the way they live their lives in the future.

The identity that you provide as a father should cause your children to be proud to carry your name and be identified with it. Jesus said, *"I and My Father are one"* (John 10:30).

When Philip asked Jesus in John 14:8 to show them the Father, Jesus' response in verse 9 was, *"Have I been with you so long, and yet you have not known Me, Philip? He who has seen Me has seen the Father; so how can you say, 'Show us the Father?'"*

Jesus was so identified with His Father that when asked, "Where are you from?" Jesus said, "I am of My Father and you are of your father the devil" (see John 8:25-44). Jesus would not be identified as being from Bethlehem, or Nazareth or Capernaum; He would not be identified as being the son of Mary and Joseph.

Jesus told His questioners that He was of His Father who is in heaven. He said, *"...I must be about My Father's business"* (Luke 2:49). A son always was identified with his father's business, and Jesus was no exception. He took His identity from His Father and in His Father's name (identity), He went about doing good.

So it is today. Every one of us receives our identity from our fathers for good or for bad. Fathers are progenitors (producers of genes or generations); their identities are passed on to the third and fourth generations. So, fathers, let me ask you, what kind of identity, what kind of mark, what kind of legacy is your name passing on to your children?

PROVIDING UNITY FOR YOUR FAMILY

Fathers are also to provide unity in their family, their church and their community. The father is created and called by God to be the one who holds things together and does not allow things to fall apart. One of the tragedies of our day is the breakdown of the family and the rise in the number of matriarchal controlled and dominated households.

When I grew up, we had to look to our mother many times to hold everything together. This placed a tremendous burden on her—a burden that she was not created to bear. And although my mother and many other mothers have borne this burden in the heat of the day, mothers were never created to carry the load of being the source of provision, identity or unity. That role and that responsibility rest squarely on the shoulders of fathers.

Fathers are needed in the home to be crisis managers. Living together in a family can be trying and often involves conflict. Through the wisdom given them, fathers must know how to creatively resolve the conflicts that often confront families. They teach their families how to respect the space of other members of the family. Fathers must help each member of their families realize and accept the fact that they are not in the family to be served but to serve one another. When misunderstandings happen fathers who understand the power of the father force do not ignore them, hoping that they will go away. They jump into the middle of the conflict and bring peaceful resolution.

The father in the home is to provide the stability that unites and holds everything together. The word *husband* means, "house band." He is the band, which holds the house firmly in place, united and stable.

Fathers produce unity in the home by the way they understand and treat with respect each person in the family, especially their wives. Fathers, it is important for you to learn what motivates and what encourages each child and then supply that generously and without partiality. We must study the traits and characteristics of our families and know how to move each of them to consensus to do what is best for the common good of the family as a unit. We produce a climate of unity by the way we speak to and treat our children's mother. If the children sense disrespect of the mother from the father, it will create a potential schism within the family unit. Children will be forced to take sides, and this is one of the tragedies of divorce and broken family relationships.

Fathers have the force, the power, to hold things together and to create a harmony and unity within the family structure that will last forever.

PROVIDING DESTINY FOR YOUR FAMILY

Fathers who understand the force of fatherhood will provide direction for the children in their homes. Many children today are struggling with what to do with their lives; turning to gangs and violence, drugs and premarital sex primarily because they have no father who can give them any sense of direction. Good fathers know how to help their families discover their gifts and abilities. They know how to breathe vision into their children's lives. As they help them discover their gifts, they then provide direction in the development of those gifts. They will actively get their children involved in activities that will teach them life skills that will serve them in their adult lives. Through their direction and encouragement fathers give their children the courage and passion to be more than they ever imagined they could be. Fathers should actively encourage every effort their children make in order to increase their self-confidence.

Good fathers will link their families to the heavenly Father, who will reveal His ultimate plans for their lives. A good father will teach his family how to hear the voice of God and encourage them to follow His voice, no matter how challenging that word might be.

The apostle Paul said in 1 Corinthians 4:15, *For though you might have ten thousand instructors in Christ, yet you do not have many fathers.... Instructors* in that verse carries the meaning of "boy teachers," those who teach you boyhood things or childhood things. Children have man-teachers who are attempting to teach them the way to go, how to make a living and what fields they should pursue in life. But instructors cannot give our children what a father can—that is a sense of their true destiny in Christ. The force of a father can alter the destructive destiny that a child may be traveling toward through wrong choices and bad decisions.

Without fathers it is difficult to have a sense of direction and destiny. Just as Jesus said to His followers, *"Follow Me..."* (Matthew 4:19), and as Paul told his sons and daughters in the faith to ...*imitate me* (1 Corinthians 4:16), so too, fathers can say to their children, "follow me and imitate me." This is something a teacher cannot give—destiny.

A man that God blesses is a father who will be able to effectively provide for his family a sense of true identity and divine destiny. Getting into the place where the blessings flow will result in an overflow for his family. Who is the man that God blesses?

THE MAN GOD BLESSES DOES NOT HAVE A LOSER'S LIMP

God is calling fathers and men *from* the church, *into* the community, *into* the marketplace, the social and political institutions, and *into* our homes! However, becoming the kind of man God is looking for, the kind of man He blesses, involves much more than just being a male. It also requires more than just being a churchman.

There are a growing number of fathers and men who avoid their responsibilities because of what I call the "loser's limp." That is what happens when a football player tries to

GOD IS LOOKING FOR KINGDOM MEN WHO UNDERSTAND THAT THEY HAVE THE "FORCE OF FATHERHOOD," MEN WHO ARE NOT OVERCOME BY THE WORLD BUT WHO SEEK TO TRANSFORM AND OVERCOME THE WORLD!

catch a pass but because of his misjudgment he misses the ball. He doesn't want anyone to know that he blew it, so he falls down and gets up limping to hide his failure. The "loser's limp" is what happens when a runner who is favored to win is getting

dusted in the 100-meter or 200-meter race, so he comes up limping with a sudden muscle pull or cramp.

The "loser's limp" is the way some fathers camouflage failure. And far too many men today are camouflaging their failure to be the kind of men God blesses! They are suffering from "excusitis." As a pastor I hear these excuses all the time: "It's the way I was raised," or "My father left my mother," or "It's because of this woman I have," or "Everybody else is doing it," or "My job demands so much time." But no matter what a man's excuses may be for failing to fulfill his divine, God-given role, the fact remains that he is not getting the job done. When he is not getting the job done, he will not be able to successfully provide for all the needs of his family.

Author Les T. Csorba, former White House advisor for presidential personnel, has a name for fathers who suffer from the loser's limp and excusitis. Csorba calls them "Phantom Fathers" in his book *Trust: The One Thing That Makes or Breaks a Leader.* They are either out of sight or in sight but checked out. He cites a story told by family expert, Dr. James Dobson. The Dobson's second son arrived just as Dr. Dobson's popularity skyrocketed following the success of his book, *Dare to Discipline.* He was asked to appear on talk shows, travel to promote his new book, and present "question-and-answer" forums for parents to learn how to parent.

Already a busy college professor, Dobson was soon overwhelmed. Then he received a life-changing letter from his own father. Dobson says:

> *My father, who always served as a beacon in dark times, saw what was happening to me and wrote a letter that was to change my life. First, he congratu-*

lated me on my success, but then warned that all the success in the world would not compensate if I failed at home. He reminded me that the spiritual welfare of our children was my most important responsibility, and that the only way to build their faith was to model it personally and then to stay on my knees in prayer. That couldn't be done if I invested every resource in my profession.

Dr. Dobson resigned from the university and developed a ministry that allowed him to stay at home more often. He turned down requests to speak and began his radio program. Travel was no longer an issue. He did it all to honor his relationship with his wife and children (who are now leaders in their own right), while launching *Focus on the Family*, one of the most influential family ministries in the world. Dr. Dobson says, "The relationship with those you love will outweigh every other good thing in your life."

THE MAN WHO GOD BLESSES IS NOT MISSING IN ACTION

Excuses do not change the facts, and the fact is that too many fathers are missing in action. Surveys estimate that 41 percent of all American children go to bed without a father in the home to pray with them or tuck them in. In the African-American and Hispanic communities, that figure rises to almost 65 percent, and by the year 2010, it is estimated that this number could climb to approximately 70 percent.

It is also a fact that 46 percent of children raised in single-mother households live below poverty level. There is no father there to provide for them. Records show that 57 percent of state prison inmates grew up without a father in the home, and 70 percent of all rapists come from fatherless homes. And 18 million children in America are entitled to more than 34 billion dollars in child support, with 90 percent of that being from fathers who are not in the home.

No matter what the social engineers, sociologists, and others have to say, and no matter how the feminists feel or what the radical liberal agenda trumpets as the answer—the world is still in a mess. This world is suffering not from a "Godlessness Problem" but from a "Fatherlessness Problem." And no amount of government spending, social reform, welfare reform or any other kind of reform can solve the lingering pattern of destruction in our world today. Our problems can only be resolved by the restoration, revival, and spiritual renewal of fatherhood. The power to transform our world— is the father force!

THE MAN WHO GOD BLESSES WILL STAND AGAINST THE TIDE

It is time for men to stand up in our sin-sick world and be the kingdom fathers and men who make a positive difference. The blessings of God are at stake; the health, wealth, and salvation of our families and all the families of the earth are on the line and hanging in the balance.

We must understand that Satan knows the value and importance of men and fathers. The Bible clearly shows that whenever Satan wanted to destroy a civilization and attempt to stop the plan of God's kingdom, he went after the male seed. Sodom and Gomorrah perished because Satan perverted the men to lust after other men, rather than to love, cherish and marry women. In the Old Testament, Pharaoh, king of

Egypt, gave orders to have the midwives kill the male Hebrew children who were born during the time of Moses. The pattern continued in the time of our Lord Jesus. King Herod wanted to destroy all the male children, hoping to kill the One who was born King of the Jews, the Christ child.

Satan's plan has not been changed. He understands the power of the father force, and he is still seeking to destroy the male seed by polluting the minds and spirits of men with drugs, alcohol, pornography, homosexuality and lustful perversions. Satan has used the traps of sin to literally emasculate a generation of men, feminize others, and silence the voices of still others with guilt, shame and low self-esteem.

Today there seems to be a spiritual fog that has descended over many fathers and men, and it extends even to those in the church. Someone once observed that a fog covering six city blocks contains approximately one glass of water. In other words, fog is a lot of smoke but has very little substance. This is a vivid description of the situation we are facing in the church—not only in America but around the world. This is a clear picture of the state of fatherhood and manhood in many communities as it relates to fathers and men, understanding the responsibility and force they are for social, political, economic and spiritual change.

However, it does not have to be this way. If fathers of every race, color and heritage could and would unite and stand together against this "equal opportunity" onslaught of the devil and stand against the tide of deterioration of the family, it would release a force of power so awesome that it would transform our world, and we could begin to experience what God placed Adam on earth for—to bring His kingdom to the earth as it is in heaven.

God has an exciting, challenging and fulfilling Kingdom agenda for fathers specifically and men in general. He desires and longs to bless fathers and men so that His blessing will flow through them into the lives of their families and their children, and on to their children's children. It is time for fathers to start walking in that divine blessing and living it out in their daily lives.

THE MAN THAT GOD BLESSES KNOWS THE POWER OF GOD

The man God blesses knows beyond a shadow of a doubt that there is no other name or power like Jesus, no other king like the King of kings, the King of glory. Stephen lived in such a way that God blessed him with the highest compliment given to any man other than Enoch, who walked so intimately with God until God walked Him into the glory of eternity without Enoch passing through death. Stephen, whose story is found in Acts 6-8, was such a man of vision, virtue, values and faith that when he died serving the Lord and witnessing about the Kingdom of God, Jesus honored him in such a way that it has never been duplicated. The Lord Jesus Christ did not sit down and receive this great father and man into glory—Jesus stood up and gave Stephen a standing ovation (see Acts 6-8).

Fathers, will you so live as a kingdom man in life and in death—in defeat and in victory? Will you live in such a way as to have Jesus standing up cheering you on? If so, you will hear the cheers of heaven welcoming you into His kingdom. If so, you are the man that God will bless in all you do!

That blessing will be a great provision for the future of your family.

A VISION FOR YOUR FAMILY—YOUR GREATEST PROVISION

God originally gave Adam the vision and the command to provide direction and destiny for those who would come after him. God gave Adam the direct command; Adam was the recipient of all the information, the revelation and the communication from God. God's purpose was to have an orderly transfer of His commands from Adam [father] to all those who were of his family.

A father who has no God-given vision for life will destroy his family quicker than anything from the outside. Proverbs 29:18 KJV says, *Where there is no vision, the people perish....* That verse is literally translated, where there is no revelation from God, the people cast off restraints. Which is to say that when the father has no vision from God for his family, that family will cast off restraints, boundaries and lower their standards and accept anything as legitimate.

The vision for a harmonious society, the vision of dominion and replenishment and continual fellowship with God was given to fathers through the person of Adam. It is the responsibility of fathers to keep this vision alive and to transfer this vision into the lives of their children and their children's children.

When fathers lack vision (a clear mental picture of a preferable future for their families); when fathers lack a clear mental picture of their families living in the will of God and living out the purpose of God for them...their families will perish. Father, your family may not perish physically—but before your very eyes you will witness a lowering of standards in your children, and it will continue until you provide the vision, the revelation and the clear picture of what your family is going to be under the leadership of the Holy Spirit. Father, you have access to the throne of God the Father (if you are born again) and you have been given the power (the force of fatherhood). Therefore you should stay before God in prayer, seeking His vision for your family. Get in His Word (the Bible) and seek a fresh rhema word, a living word for you and your family. Then write the vision and make it plain, so that when your wife and children read it they can run with it and bring it to pass. You are the provider of vision for your family.

This is destiny…this is the role of a provider.

FATHER REFLECTIONS

1. *What is your "loser's limp"? How can you begin today to more effectively provide for the needs of your family?*

2. *What is your God-given vision for your life as a man…for your family? In what specific ways are you transferring that vision to your family, particularly to your children?*

3. *Can you recall one of your favorite childhood moments? Was your father in or out of the picture? How will you begin to create life-changing, identity-driven memories for your children?*

4. *If you died at this very moment, what kind of reception would you receive from the Lord Jesus Christ? Would you receive a standing ovation like Stephen?*

CHAPTER SIX

Father—Why Do We Long to Cry in His Arms?

"He is a high priest who can be touched with the feelings of our infirmities."

Fulfilling a spiritual role in the family requires fathers to be spiritual. You cannot deliver to others what you have not received. Speaking to God and hearing from God demands a certain spirituality that is not attained overnight. The root word for spirituality is *spirit*. Effective fathers must be men of the Spirit. The Holy Spirit is given to them to empower them and to guide them. Men, you are not alone. When Jesus ascended to His Father He promised that He would send the Comforter, the Alongside One, who would be with you at all times and who would guide you into all truth. He would be the Communicator on behalf of God. By His presence He will help you to fulfill your role as priest and prophet in your family.

A Spirit-filled Man

And Jesus, full of the Holy Spirit, returned from the Jordan and was led about by the Spirit in the wilderness for forty days, being tempted by the devil. And He ate nothing during those days; and when they had ended, He became hungry. And the devil said to Him, "If You are the Son of God, tell this stone to become bread." And Jesus answered him, "It is written, 'Man shall not live on bread alone.'" And he led Him up and showed Him all the kingdoms of the world in a moment of time. And the devil said to Him, "I will give You all this domain and its glory; for it has been handed over to me, and I give it to whomever I wish. Therefore if You worship before me, it shall all be Yours." And Jesus answered and said to him, "It is written, 'You shall worship the Lord your God and serve Him only.'" And he led Him to Jerusalem and had Him stand on the pinnacle of the temple, and said to Him, "If You are the Son of God, throw Yourself down from here; for it is written, 'He will give His angels charge concerning You to guard You, and, on their hands they will bear You up, lest You strike Your foot against a stone.'" And Jesus answered and said to him, "It is said, 'You shall not put the Lord your God to the test.'" And when the devil had finished every temptation, he departed from Him until an opportune time. And Jesus returned to Galilee in the power of the Spirit; and news about Him spread through all the surrounding district.

—Luke 4:1-14 NASB

The Holy Spirit is our *helper*, the *other comforter*, sent by the Father to continue the work of Jesus. Jesus' work was finished on earth, and He is seated at the right hand of the Father ever making intercession for you and me. The Holy Spirit has now come into the world and permanently dwells in the lives of every born-again believer. He has come to be to us everything that Jesus was to the apostles and early disciples during His earthly ministry. Just as Jesus told His disciples, *"...without Me you can do nothing"* (John 15:5), the same holds true in our relationship with the Holy Spirit. Without the Holy Spirit actively leading, guiding, teaching, helping, comforting, rebuking, protecting and providing for us, we can do nothing worthwhile for the kingdom of God. Of grave importance is the fact that unless we, as fathers, submit and surrender to the leading of the Holy Spirit, we will be unable to fulfill our spiritual role in the family.

THE WORLD AND ITS FAMILIES NEED FATHERS WHO ARE MEN OF THE SPIRIT

I have a hunger, thirst, and burning desire to be continuously filled with the Spirit of Christ so I can be like Philip of the Bible, who literally died to his own personal needs, desires, wishes, visions and dreams. I want to be filled with the Spirit of Christ Jesus to the point that I only desire what our Heavenly Father desires.

I am burdened about the lack of desperation, hunger and thirst for the things of God in the lives of men today. God's plan is for men to be living examples for their wives, children, co-workers, friends, and relatives. God has called men to be leaders in this world. Fathers are called to be examples of what it means to be saints and bold soldiers in the Lord's army.

Wives need Spirit-filled husbands, and children need Spirit-filled fathers. The business world has enough men filled with the spirit of greed, competition and treachery—*the business world needs Spirit-filled businessmen.* The whole world is anxious to see real spiritual men and fathers arise—in the entertainment world, the sports world, the arts, the sciences, education, law and government. Too many men are filled with the spirit of lust, envy, rebellion, pride, wickedness, materialism, perversion and sexual immorality. Where are the spiritual fathers who can heal the crises in the home and the conflicts in our world?

What the world needs in each of these arenas of life is an infiltration of men of God who are saved, sanctified and filled with the Spirit of the Lord Jesus Christ—fathers and men who will stand boldly and show those who are lost and in danger of hell that Jesus Christ is Lord of all. One of the reasons we are not experiencing this kind of spiritual boldness and leadership from fathers is because the church is lacking in the number of men who are filled with the Spirit of God. What the world and the church need today are more men who will be spiritual fathers to those men and boys in the church whose lives are spiritually shallow and religiously bound. We need fathers filled with the Spirit of Jesus Christ, the fullness of the Godhead, the Spirit of power and of love and of a sound mind. For men to live by the Spirit and be filled with the Spirit, it is crucial for fathers to understand what is required to become a Spirit-filled man.

WHAT IS A SPIRIT-FILLED MAN?

Jesus is our primary example of what it means to be a Spirit-filled man. Luke 4:1 says, *Then Jesus, being filled with* *the Holy Spirit, returned from the Jordan and was <u>led by the</u> <u>Spirit</u> into the wilderness* (emphasis added).

To be filled with the Spirit, or to be Spirit-filled, first means that you are saved; that the Holy Spirit has come into your life and has taken up permanent residence. He lives in you because you are saved. Every man who is saved has been filled with the Spirit and will not get any more of the Spirit than he already has. So the issue then becomes, **how much of your life does the Holy Spirit control?** To be filled with the Spirit, or to be Spirit-filled, also means you are totally surrendered to the gentle yet firm leading of the Holy Spirit. It means that you allow the Holy Spirit to have complete control over your heart and your mind. A father who is filled with the Spirit allows the Holy Spirit within to invade every crack and crevice of his being—his thoughts, motives, words, deeds, dreams, goals, and his relationships with his wife, his children and with other people. The Holy Spirit is a part of his dreams, his goals, his business and his leisure.

If you are a Spirit-filled man, the Holy Spirit will reign supreme over your will, your emotions and your intelligence, but not without your permission. A Spirit-filled man is to be filled to the point of saturation; a fullness that leaves nothing else to be desired. Your life will exemplify the free and unhindered exercise of all the Holy Spirit's attributes— His knowledge, His power, His holiness, His peace and His joy.

Look at these Spirit-filled men in the Bible and the characteristics they revealed. We need to see these characteristics in the lives of God's men and fathers today.

Boldness

> Then Peter, filled with the Holy Spirit...began to speak the word of God with boldness.
> —Acts 4:8; 31 NASB

Heavenly Vision

> But being full of the Holy Spirit, he [Stephen] gazed intently into heaven and saw the glory of God, and Jesus standing at the right hand of God.
> —Acts 7:55 NASB

> Set your mind on the things above, not on the things that are on earth.
> —Colossians 3:2 NASB

Faith

> He [Barnabas] was a good man, and full of the Holy Spirit and of faith.
> —Acts 11:24 NASB

Authority

> ...Paul, filled with the Holy Spirit, fixed his gaze upon him [Elymas], and said... "And now, behold, the hand of the Lord is upon you, and you will be blind and not see the sun for a time." And immediately a mist and a darkness fell upon him, and he went about seeking those who would lead him by the hand.
> —Acts 13:9, 11 NASB

Joy

> And the disciples were continually filled with joy and with the Holy Spirit.
> —Acts 13:52 NASB

How to become a Spirit-filled man

Jesus is God, and He does not need anyone or anything. He is Lord of all. He is King of kings and therefore He does not need the help of the Holy Spirit. So why would Jesus, God in the flesh, need to come under the control of the Holy Spirit? Jesus could handle the devil, temptations and life because He was God! Indeed Jesus was God, but He was also a man.

Entering into our world, He stripped Himself of every heavenly advantage, and He walked among us in the flesh. He knew that to fulfill the Father's will He must be empowered by the Spirit of His Father. More importantly, Jesus did it to set an example for you and me. Jesus knows that as men, we have a tendency to think that we can do anything. We think there is nothing we cannot handle on our own. However, the truth is we must totally and completely surrender our lives to God.

Totally and completely surrender your life to God

Jesus shows us that the first step toward becoming a "Spirit-filled man," is to be totally and completely surrendered to The Father. The Bible says He was led by the Spirit. Being led by someone means being surrendered to their leadership—surrendering to their direction, their control and their will. It suggests that you have yielded control over the direction of your life. Their will is in control of where you go, what you do, when you do what you do and how you do it.

Fathers must not continue to live the same lifestyle, talk the same talk and walk the same walk. You cannot continue to try to figure everything out and make everything work, and cover up mistakes and wrongs when you know that you don't have it all together. You know that at any moment you can lose it and your life will fall apart. As long as you are full of your own ego, pride, and self-will and as long as you believe that you can handle your marriage, your business, your career, your children, your emotions, your sexuality and on and on, the Holy Spirit will continue to let you live on the roller coaster of uncertainty.

After being born again, the first step to being a Spirit-filled man is to recognize that you cannot handle life by yourself. This takes great humility and a relinquishing of pride (male ego). Most of us have tried it on our own, but have found out that life just doesn't work the way we plan it. There must come a point in your life—and it will come—when you will get so desperate that you can't do anything else in your own strength and you will be broken and willing to do anything, including surrendering to the Holy Spirit. As long as you struggle, the Holy Spirit will let you struggle. As long as you insist on doing it your way, you will continue to fail, because to rededicate means that you simply commit to trying harder to do something that you are capable of doing.

The Spirit-filled man is *a surrendered man*. He is one who says, *"I cannot make it on my own. I cannot be the kind of husband, father, preacher, businessman, friend, worker or teacher that God wants me to be unless I get help."* And Jesus said the Helper, the Holy Spirit, is here for you. He is available not only to help you after you surrender, but to help you surrender.

BECOME TOTALLY DEPENDENT ON THE HOLY SPIRIT

To be a Spirit-filled man is to become ***totally dependent on the Holy Spirit***. If you study the New Testament, it is easy to notice that Jesus had nothing—He owned absolutely nothing. He had no food to depend on for physical strength. He had no friends to depend on for emotional or moral support. He had no transportation except for his two feet. He had no map for the journey and no compass to guide Him. When you surrender to someone, it stands to reason that you must become totally and completely dependent upon him for everything you need. Now, Jesus could have had everything…and indeed He did have everything He needed through the help of the women who ministered to Him out of their own substance, through the help of those who believed in Him and furnished homes for Him to rest in and all His earthly needs. But in actuality Jesus was not dependent upon what others did for Him; He was dependent upon the Holy Spirit leading Him and His Father providing for Him.

If you are going to become a Spirit-filled father and man of God, you not only must surrender to the Holy Spirit, but you must also become totally dependent on Him. You must depend on Him to help you overcome the temptation to sin, to feed you when you are hungry and to put you in your proper place in life. You must depend on Him to guide you into truth and to keep you from falling. When you depend on the Holy Spirit to help you become the father and man of God that He created you to be, your family will be blessed, your church will be enriched and your community will be made better.

Fathers and men, stop trying to live the Christian life and be a good father, husband or friend, and start depending on the Holy Spirit to lead you into what God wants for you and for your family. Stop struggling with the Spirit of God; surrender to and depend on Him to cause you to obey the voice of God, to live victoriously and to reflect the person of Jesus Christ.

Have you ever found yourself begging, bargaining and pleading with God for a spiritual change in your life? Or have you ever felt the need to work harder in the church in order to please God so that He would give in to your requests? Have you ever been frustrated because you wanted so much to be filled with the Holy Spirit, but you didn't know how to go about it?

Today you can be filled with the fullness and the overflowing presence of the Holy Spirit. Are you willing to become totally dependent and surrendered to God so the Holy Spirit can maximize His work in your life? If you are, God will manifest His Spirit in you as never before, and the force of fatherhood will flow from you as a river of living water.

FATHERS ARE PRIESTS IN THEIR OWN HOME

As we have already indicated, there is a great need for fathers to take their responsible place within their families, their churches and their communities. We live in a time when too many fathers have not given attention to their needed place. There are too many who have abandoned the home and left mothers to raise their children. They have abandoned the church and left women to run the church. Even those who have not abandoned their families have not

effectively fulfilled their most important roles in the family—
to be the priests in their homes.

The reason fathers have abandoned the role of priest in
the home and the church is because many, if not most, men
do not know how to be priests. A priest in the home represents the family before
God. A priest makes intercession for others. Just as
Jesus is our High Priest,
seated at the right hand of
the Father, ever making
intercession for us, so too the
father is the priest who
stands in the presence of Christ on behalf of his family. And
here is the key—he makes himself available as the answer for
the meeting of their needs.

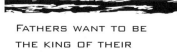

FATHERS WANT TO BE
THE KING OF THEIR
CASTLE, BUT UNTIL THEY
ARE WILLING TO SERVE
AS PRIEST, THEY ARE
NOT WORTHY TO BE KING.

The greatest role a priest has is that of intercessor. If
every father would earnestly intercede for his children, the
father force would literally turn our world around instanta-
neously. A father who understands the force of fatherhood
will be awakened to and aware of the powerful weapon of
prayer, and he will use it continually on behalf of his children
and his children's children. When a husband understands his
force of fatherhood and the power of prayer, he will lay on
his face before God on behalf of his wife and the needs that
she has in her life.

A father teaches his children to pray by praying *for*
them and praying *with* them. By his example he will show
them the importance of prayer. Five Star General Douglas
MacArthur, the famous American hero of World War II, put
it this way:

By profession I am a soldier and take pride in that fact. But I am prouder —infinitely prouder—to be a father. A soldier destroys in order to build; the father only builds, never destroys. The one has the potentiality of death; the other embodies creation and life. And while the hordes of death are mighty, the battalions of life are mightier still. It is my hope that my son, when I am gone, will remember me not from the battle field but in the home repeating with him our simple daily prayer, Our Father Who Art in Heaven.

As priests in the home, fathers can literally turn their hearts to their children. Children need someone who they know beyond a doubt will pray for them, lead them into spiritual truth and help them make spiritual decisions. The Bible says in Hebrews 4:14-15 that we have a *great High Priest…Jesus the Son of God…We do not have a High Priest who cannot sympathize with our weaknesses…* Jesus knows how to pray for us and can sympathize with our feelings of weakness because verse 15 goes on to say, …[He] *was in all points tempted as we are, yet without sin.*

Who better to pray and intercede for you than some-one who has walked in your shoes and who has traveled the road that you now travel? A father is in the perfect position as priest to pray for his children because he has been where they are right now. He was tempted with drugs, sexual immorality, peer pressure, violence, music, smoking, drinking, partying and every other vice his child is being tempted with today.

Unfortunately, some fathers have fallen into some of these vices, but God has graciously brought them out and cleansed them with the precious blood of Christ. Therefore we can sympathize with our children's time of weakness, and as their intercessors—rather than judge them and condemn them—we can pray fervently on their behalf that God would be as gracious to them as He has been to us.

FATHERS AS PROPHETS

The father is not only the priest in the lives of his family members but also the prophet. A priest is one who goes before God on behalf of someone else. A prophet is one who comes to someone on behalf of God. As a prophet a father is to declare God's Word to his family.

Fathers are to "forth tell" the Word of God to their families—their wives and children. According to the Word of God, they are to exhort and encourage their families to live lives of holiness and to walk worthy of their calling. Fathers who have gone to God on behalf of their families must now come to their families on behalf of God. They are to let their families know what God expects of them and what they have heard and learned in their prayer closets as they sought the will of God. In the prayer closets fathers see (a prophet is a seer) God's vision for their families' lives and are then able to encourage and direct them toward God's purposes.

It was Adam who was to tell Eve, *thus said the Lord.* Adam was to be the prophet in the garden and he was to bring God's Word into reality and manifestation. He was to listen to God, not to his wife, when it came time to make the decision to eat of the tree of the knowledge of good and evil. Unfortunately, Adam decided to abdicate his position of prophet and abandon his place of spiritual leadership.

Far too many fathers are taking the same posture of abandoning the spiritual instruction of their children. Father, you may not have abandoned your family physically, but have you abandoned them spiritually? Too many fathers are leaving the teaching of the Word of God, the praying to God, the promoting of godly morals and values and the worship of God to their wives. Father, you are the force of God in the home; you are to be the prophet in the home, leading your family in worship, praise and thanksgiving to God. Fathers are to lead their families in the study of God's Word, in witnessing to the lost and in sharing in missions.

Unless fathers rise up and become more than Sunday morning visitors to the House of God, our children will become a generation that does not know the Lord. The Bible warns us in Proverbs 30 that this generation, who knows more about MTV, BET, VH-1, iPODS and Cyberspace than about the things of God, would be a generation that is totally rebellious and violently lost.

> *There is a generation that curses its father, and does not bless its mother. There is a generation that is pure in its own eyes, yet is not washed from its filthiness. There is a generation—oh, how lofty are their eyes! And their eyelids are lifted up. There is a generation whose teeth are like swords, and whose fangs are like knives, to devour the poor from off the earth, and the needy from among men.*
> —Proverbs 30:11-14

This is that generation that needs prophetic fathers who will impart spiritual truth and godly wisdom into their lives. Now is not the time to shy away from this generation;

rather, now is the time to become like the prophets of old who were consumed with their message and passionate about being faithful to deliver what the Lord was saying. The prophetic force of fatherhood is the power that can transform our world.

PROPHETS OR ENTERTAINERS

I believe one of the faults of fatherhood today is that many of us, as men, have fallen in love with the world. We love being entertained by the world of sports, movies, magazines and now the world of the Internet. The result is that we are raising a self-centered, gadget-driven, computer-addicted generation of children who are hooked on entertainment. It seems as though the church has fallen into the competitive nature of entertaining rather than confronting with a clear clarion call to Christlikeness.

Many fathers have made the mistake of trying to be their children's best friend and entertainer. Father, this is not your God-given role. Your role is to be a prophet in the lives of your children, giving them focus, guidance and sound doctrinal direction. Your role is to be the voice of reason and the voice of one leading them into the Word of God and into a life that honors God.

A prophet was God's representative to His people. Fathers, you represent God to your children. The reason God said in Malachi 4 that He wanted the fathers to turn their hearts to the children and the children to turn their hearts to their fathers, was because His own children, Israel had turned their hearts away from Him and sought out other gods. They chased after the false gods of the pagan nations around them. Jesus Christ, God's Son, was sent to turn God's children back to their Father.

As fathers, when we fulfill our role as prophets to our children, we will shape their image of God by the example we provide for them. This means that we are to reveal by our very character the pattern of God and the relationship He desires to have with our children. As prophets, fathers are to be men of faith. It is your faith that you must pass on to your children. Why? Because ...*without faith it is impossible to please Him [God]...* (Hebrews 11:6), and it is by faith that they will overcome the world.

Satan attacks your home to get to your faith. When Satan attacked Job, it was for the expressed purpose of destroying Job's faith in God. But Job maintained his faith and said, *Though He slay me, yet will I trust* [have faith in] Him (Job 13:15).

Fathers, when you are under attack, that is not the time to give up and give in; that is the time to reveal to your children the power of the prophetic anointing that God has given you as a man of God. That is the time to reveal the father force within you! It is the time to say to your children, "Things are tough right now, but I trust God, and I am fully persuaded that God will grant us favor, and we will come out of this as winners."

George, my dad, always encouraged us to look to the future, even though times were tough. When we had to eat "Pork-n-Beans" and cube steaks for weeks and weeks at a time, George would constantly remind us that things would get better—that one day, because of our education and hard work, we would be able to eat whatever we wanted.

I became an expert at cooking cube steak and pork-n-beans. But when I look back at what my father taught me during those days—how to see a better tomorrow even in the midst of a dark day today and how to trust God and be thankful for what I did have—I realize now just how prophetic my father, George, really was.

Fathers, when you are consistent in your words of encouragement and affirmation, you are transferring your faith to your child and teaching them that God will never leave them nor forsake them (see Deuteronomy 31:8), and that they can always depend on the faithfulness of God. You are teaching them that they will never be forsaken nor will they have to beg for bread (see Psalm 37:25).

When your wife and children see a demonstration of your faith in the tough times of life, it prepares them to go through the storms, through the fires and through the valley of the shadow of death, with confidence in God, confidence in themselves and confidence in you as their priest and their prophet.

FATHERS AS ENCOURAGERS

The story is told of a young boy who was playing soccer. He could not have been any more than five, maybe six years of age, but he and his teammates were playing for the championship of their league. To them it was a real game—a serious game. The parents were as serious as the players. They had coaches and uniforms, linesmen and referees. All eyes were on the teams as the game began.

The teams seemed to be pretty evenly matched, and in the first period no one scored on either team. The kids were hilarious! They were clumsy and terribly inefficient, as only children can be. They fell over their own feet, they stumbled over the ball, they kicked the ball and missed it, but they didn't seem to mind. They were just having fun and enjoying playing the game! In the second period, the coach pulled out all of his first team so that players on his second team could have a chance to play. That was the rule of the league, that all the children must have a chance to play.

But it seemed like the coach of the opposing team did not abide by the rules of the game. He refused to take out his first team because he wanted to win, and the parents demanded that they win! At this point the game took a dramatic turn. A young boy, whose parents were in the stands watching, was put in as the goalie. Because of the advantage of the opponents, they began to score on him. One goal after another; he could not stop the barrage of shots coming at him. He was a good player for a five or six-year-old, but he was no match for three or four on the other team who were equally as good. The goalie gave it his all. He recklessly threw his body in front of incoming balls, trying valiantly to stop them, but the other team kept scoring quickly and repeatedly.

It infuriated the young boy, and he became a raging maniac—shouting, running and diving. With all his might and all the strength he could muster, he finally was able to cover one of the boys on the other team as he approached the goal. But that boy kicked the ball to another boy twenty feet away, and by the time the young goalie could reposition himself, it was too late. They scored another goal.

His parents were looking on. They were nice, decent-looking people. His father looked as though he had just rushed over to the game from the office. He still had on his suit and tie. The parents yelled encouragement to their son. But after the fourth and fifth goal, the little boy changed. He could see it was no use; he couldn't stop the other team. He didn't quit, but he became quietly desperate, and futility and frustration was written all over his face.

His father changed too. He had been urging his son to try harder, yelling advice and encouragement. But then he became anxious. He tried to yell out to his son that it was okay, encouraging him to hang in there. But as a father, he grieved for the pain his son was feeling. After the sixth and seventh goals, the little boy needed help so badly, but there was no help to be had.

He retrieved the ball from the net and handed it to the referee; then he just broke down and cried. He stood there while huge tears rolled down both cheeks. He went to his knees—and that is when his father started onto the field.

The mother tried to stop him. She thought that he was angry with the boy and that he would yell at him and embarrass him even more! But he tore loose from her and ran onto the field. He wasn't supposed to, for the game was still in progress. Suit, tie, dress shoes, and all—he charged onto the field and picked up his son so everybody would know that this was his boy. And he hugged him and kissed him—and cried with him.

He carried him off the field, and when they got close to the sidelines he said to his son, "Jimmy, I'm so proud of you. You were great out there. I want everybody to know that you are my son."

"Daddy," the boy sobbed, "I couldn't stop them. I tried, Daddy, I tried and tried but they kept scoring on me."

"Jimmy, it doesn't matter how many times they score on

you. You're my son, and I'm proud of you. I want you to go back out there and finish the game. I know you want to quit, but you can't. And, son, you're going to get scored on again, but it doesn't matter. You are still my son!"

It made a great deal of difference as little Jimmy ran back on to the field. His confidence was restored and his self-image was intact, because he knew that his identity was not determined by his performance. And, yes, the other team scored two more times; but, it was okay—he knew the power of his father's encouragement, and that changed the situation!

A father's encouragement can affect a child's attitude about himself or herself for a lifetime. You will never know what courageous leadership on your part will do to prepare your children to face life with courage and grace.

FATHER REFLECTIONS

1. *Who interceded for you as you were growing up? How have their prayers impacted your life today? Have you thanked them?*

2. *What hinders your prayer life? Do you feel that you are taking the responsibility of praying for your children seriously enough?*

3. *Why do you feel that studying the Word of God is critical to you becoming an effective prophet in your home?*

4. *What image of God do your children have, based on your example?*

CHAPTER SEVEN

Father—What Makes Him a Courageous Leader?

"He is our leader, our hero."

To deal with the growing stress and pressures caused by fatherlessness in our society, it will take fathers who are men of courage to stand and give the leadership that is necessary to bring about a change.

- *An average of 3.751 marriages in America end in divorce each day.*

- *America's divorce rate is now more than double what it was in 1960.*

- *One million children a year see their parents divorce.*

- *More than 50 percent of the children in America's public schools live in single-parent households.*

- *35 percent of America's children live apart from their biological fathers.*

- *50 percent of children who live apart from their biological fathers have never set foot in their father's house.*

- *Children in single-parent homes have a 300 percent greater possibility of negative life outcome than children raised in homes where both parents are present.*

- *In the past 40 years, pregnancies out of wedlock have increased 600 percent.*

- *In less than 40 years, cohabitation, shacking up or living together without being married has increased 1,000 percent.*

- *Less than 40 percent of married couples say they are happy.*

- *Among evangelicals, Internet pornography is now one of the leading factors in the dissolution of families and departure from ministry.*

What is the solution? Is there any power that can change the course of our time? I believe that God in His divine and sovereign wisdom prepared the answer before we could ask the question. The father force is the power that God has placed within fathers and men to impact the culture, the community, the church and the family in a positive manner. It is the power that God gave to each man to be like Him.

What makes God Father? There was a time when God was God—but He was not Father. God was and has always been self-sufficient and in need of nothing and no one. God had within Him all of Him…Father, Son and Holy Spirit. However it was not until God spoke and released His Son— when *the Word became flesh and dwelt among us…* (John 1:14)—that He became Father in a visible sense. God's power, His force to create, was released through His Son. *In the beginning was the Word, and the Word was with God, and the Word was God.…All things were made through Him, and without Him nothing was made that was made* (John 1:1,3).

It was when God spoke and released His seed (Son) into the world that He became Father, and through His Son (Jesus Christ) the Father began to transform the world and redeem mankind by establishing His Kingdom and His reign on earth as it is in heaven.

The father force is that same power that God has placed within men to release our most potent weapons on this world and that is our godly seed…our sons and daughters who can change the world. When a father releases his God-given potential and walks in God's intended purpose for his life—the original design—it causes others, especially his family, to respond to the presence and the purposes of God in a positive manner.

THE BEST OF TIMES, THE WORST OF TIMES

We are living in the best of times and the worst of times. We are living in a day and time when we are seeing and experiencing great prosperity, wealth and abundance as never before in our history. We are seeing the expansion of business, the growth in housing starts and many other economic indicators are on the rise. Yet we are living in the worst of times based on the statistics cited earlier and the fact that gang violence is rising, and the radical homosexual agenda is openly and aggressively implemented using the nation's courts to legislate anti-family rulings. Abortions are increasing once again, and public schools are not a very safe place for our children or for teachers.

We are living in the best of times because we have so much in America and we have so many choices. We can travel further, faster than ever, and we can choose to go anywhere in the world virtually in a matter of seconds. Yet, as fast as we can travel and as fast as we can see the world—that is how fast our morals, our values and our sense of family stability and hope seem to be fading away.

There is a sense of calm before the storm. It is as if our national and world leadership is taking the position that *"If we don't say anything about the conditions of our lives, the fragileness of our families, the critical nature of our communities and the crises condition of our churches—perhaps it will all just go away and we can live happily ever after."* It is as if our leaders are watching a 30-minute sitcom where all the problems are worked out before the show is over.

Despite the alarming statistics, I believe that the best is yet to come and that all things really do work together for good (see Romans 8:28). However, I do not believe that it will happen until fathers take the leadership role in dealing with the challenges of our culture.

Fathers are God's answer to the multitude of problems facing our families, our communities, our churches and our society today. Every problem in society can be traced back to a father problem and therefore a father solution.

The leadership that is required to reverse the negative reports of violence and the sickening number of deaths among young men and women due to gang activity lies within the power of fathers. The leadership that is required to slow down the rate of teen suicides and instill hope in the hearts of children abandoned to the streets lies within the power of fathers. Ordinary men, with an extraordinary love for their children, their families and their God, are the most powerful leaders on earth today. This vast army of fathers and men are the solution to the challenges we face as a society.

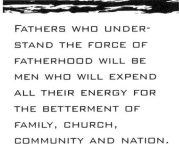

FATHERS WHO UNDER-STAND THE FORCE OF FATHERHOOD WILL BE MEN WHO WILL EXPEND ALL THEIR ENERGY FOR THE BETTERMENT OF FAMILY, CHURCH, COMMUNITY AND NATION.

While the issues of economic uncertainty, political corruption, business failures and national unrest are real, they are only symptoms of the problem. The destruction caused by drug abuse, gambling, pornography and other social ills are simply symptoms of a greater problem.

VICTIMS RATHER THAN VICTORS

The real problem is that we lack the leadership of fathers. Whether through ignorance or through neglect, too many of us have allowed our families to become victims of the world, the flesh and the devil. Many fathers that I have ministered to and counseled have allowed themselves to be caught up in the myth of inferiority, which says that other men are better than and superior to them. Therefore, these fathers and men neither expect nor demand much from themselves, and therefore, they have a sense of victimization and a license to pass the blame for their lives on to someone outside of themselves.

That is the devil's lie. It is designed to steal your creativity, your intellectual genius, your moral character and fiber, as well as your spiritual connection with the Holy Spirit. Fathers, we must understand that we are not victims of Satan, of sin, of society, of racism, of family dysfunctions, of poverty, of sickness or anything man or the devil tries to lay on us. We must abandon the victim mentality and become the kind of men we are created to be.

The challenge we face is that as fathers we have not been using ourselves up and giving ourselves up for the betterment of our families, our churches and our communities. Let's be honest and transparent. This is the reason why we are witnessing such devastation and destruction. However, whenever there is a critical need; whenever there is a crisis of faith; whenever man has come to the limits of his hope—God is faithful. God will always raise up a man who will stand in the gap and make up the hedge for the land.

> *"I believe that part of the reason for the dearth of leadership today is that we men have grown up in families where fathers did not help their children to live life courageously. Part of being a man from a biblical perspective is learning how to face your fears, to walk right toward them, and to do what is right in light of opposition. That's really all that courage is about."* [6]

---

[6] Crawford Loritts Jr., *Never Walk Away* (Moody, 1997) 141.

The urgency of the hour calls for fathers to stand courageously and take their places as the leaders in our land. The crisis of the moment calls for fathers who understand the force of fatherhood to stand courageously and go on the offensive against the moral decay. The times call for fathers to take seriously their God-given role as leadership.

For the sake of balance I do want to affirm and encourage those fathers who are doing a good job of raising their families, providing spiritual leadership for their families and being the very best dads to their children that they can be. Thank you, men of God, for being the father force.

Someone once said that all it takes for evil to triumph is for good men to do nothing. Although I salute and affirm all the good fathers of the world, imagine what would happen if all those good fathers would take a stand in the power of the father force and decide that in unity and with solidarity, they were going to lead society in an offensive attack against the vices and violence in their communities; against pornography, degrading music and videos, against abortions, drugs, alcohol and other socially unacceptable behaviors.

What would it be like if good fathers would do more than simply care for their own children and then go home and lock their doors and pray that God would not allow anyone to break into their homes or steal their BMWs, but rather become leaders against the systematic injustices that help create the climate for social chaos? What would happen if good fathers would do more than pray that their wives are not carjacked, or their child's school is not the next scene of mass murders?

What would happen if fathers of all races and faiths would collectively decide that enough is enough and set out to take back everything that has been stolen from our families?

Can you just imagine what would happen if a Moslem father would stand and demand that his 15-year-old son or his 18-year-old daughter take the bomb off of their bodies and get back in the house—enough killing? Can you just imagine what would happen if a father of a gang member would suddenly decide that enough is enough and that his son is going to take off his colors?

What would happen if the white suburban father would decide that he has given his children enough and they now need to be taught to give back to those who are less fortunate? What would happen if the absent inner-city father would return home and humbly, yet determinedly, begin to redirect the energy and the talent of his children to that which is godly?

Father, this is the father force, and it is the power that can transform the world.

Fighting to save your family

Many families are weak, defeated and struggling in poverty. Some are in debt and others lack confidence. They are being pressured into one bad choice or decision after another. Because of this many fathers are attempting to fight a spiritual war against Satan and his army of evil spirit beings with their natural minds, their natural talents and their natural emotions and wills.

A true father, a good father, will rise up against all the odds and fight for his family. These are the kinds of heroes we need in this hour—heroes who will stand up in the midst of crisis in the home and bring resolution, reform and relief.

They are not cowards in the face of battle. They will press the battle against the enemy and will preserve their family. They are the new role models for this century—heroes of another kind.

When the walls of Jerusalem were being rebuilt because the city was in ruins and the wall and the gates were torn down, Nehemiah encouraged the fathers to fight for their sons, their daughters and their wives.

> *And I looked, and arose and said to the nobles, to the leaders, and to the rest of the people, "Do not be afraid of them. Remember the Lord, great and awesome, and fight for your brethren, your sons, your daughters, your wives, and your houses."*
> —Nehemiah 4:14

The Bible clearly teaches us that we are not in a natural war. Rather, we are in a spiritual war as described in Ephesians 6:10-12. Paul describes the warfare in which you and your family are engaged as a spiritual warfare, a warfare that is taking place in heavenly places. A better word for *wrestle* is the word *war*, because you and I don't actually wrestle against these demon powers through hand-to-hand combat. Otherwise, we would not need a shield, a sword, and the other parts of the armor. We would need to be uncovered, unencumbered, loose and free to move swiftly and spontaneously. The war, the fight for our families, is a real spiritual war in which our enemy is launching missiles (thoughts) at our minds; launching fiery darts (arrows of distraction) at our lives and doing anything he can to get us to lose our hope and our faith in God. We need fathers who

will not give up in the midst of the battle but will courageously fight until the victory is attained.

Second Corinthians 10:3-4 in The Amplified Bible
reads, *For though we walk (live) in the flesh, we are not carrying on our warfare according to the flesh and using mere
human weapons. For the weapons of our warfare are not physical [weapons of flesh and blood], but they are mighty before
God for the overthrow and destruction of strongholds.*

It is critical that you know and understand how to
fight for your family and how to fight to do more than simply survive. God wants you to thrive. God wants you to
advance, to prosper and to be in health even as your soul
prospers. God's desire is for you, your children and your
children's children to live an abundant life of joy, peace and
good will. God takes pleasure in the prosperity of His children. God desires to bless you with every good thing and
cause you to be a blessing to every family on the earth.

An essential factor to receiving God's blessing is your
mindset, your attitude or your view of life. You have to
determine in your mind that you are not here on this earth
simply to get by, but that God has placed you and your family
on the earth to make a difference, to have an impact and to
change your generation. You are here to take over and not to
be overtaken!

A healthy, thriving family is critical to the balance and
preservation of the social order and structure of safety and
security for our children. A healthy, prosperous and thriving
family begins with a healthy, prosperous and thriving marriage relationship. You can be a hero to your kids by first loving
your wife. Your love for your wife will create a shield

around your children and provide a great sense of security for them.

We must never forget the fact that healthy, prosperous and thriving marriages give birth to healthy, prosperous and thriving families. Those families give birth to a healthy, prosperous and thriving church. A healthy, prosperous and thriving church gives birth to a healthy, prosperous and thriving community. A healthy, prosperous and thriving community will give birth to a nation that is healthy, prosperous and thriving! Never underestimate the responsibility you have as a father. It has worldwide implications. That is the power of the father force!

HEROES PRAY!

So how do we get there? The first step to fighting for our family is always to pray—*to seek the will and the ways of God so that we are following His plans and purposes and not trying to get God to validate our little, finite plans.* Heroes pray. They don't pray that they will be able to avoid trouble. Instead, they pray that they will be courageous and able to walk through their troubles. As Phillips Brooks, sometimes called the greatest American preacher of the nineteenth century, said, *"Do not pray for easy lives. Pray to be stronger men! Do not pray for tasks equal to your powers. Pray for power equal to your tasks."*

At the National Hispanic Prayer Breakfast, President George W. Bush emphasized the need for prayer:

> *Throughout our history, Americans of faith have always turned to prayer—for wisdom, prayer for resolve, prayers for compassion and strength, prayers*

for commitment to justice and for a spirit of forgive-
ness.

Since America's founding, prayer has reassured us
that the hand of God is guiding the affairs of this
nation. We have never asserted a special claim on His
favor, yet we've always believed in God's presence in
our lives. Prayer has comforted people in grief. Prayer
has served as a unifying factor.

Heroes have faith

As you and your family are praying, it is critical that
you understand that unless you are holding on to your faith
and using your *God-given* faith (see Romans 12:3), your
enemy will eventually wear you down and cause you to quit,
to give in and give up. He will cause you to surrender your
faith and thus lose out on the possibility of pleasing God
and being rewarded with the blessings that belong to you
already.

Ephesians 6:16 calls it the *shield of faith*, and through
the proper use of this shield you can quench, douse out, and
reject any and all fiery arrows and darts—the distractions
that are designed to destroy your faith in God, in yourself
and in your family.

You must know how to biblically apply faith to your
family life and to your family challenges and circumstances.
Understand that biblical faith is not wishful thinking. Faith
is the confidence, it is the assurance, it is the invisible reality
that lets you know that the thing you expect or hope for is
guaranteed and is going to happen.

True biblical faith is to know with assurance and complete confidence, in spite of the circumstances or situations,
that what God has said in His Word about your situation is

what you hope for or expect to happen. Because God has said it, you begin to act like you already have it.

FATHERS AND THEIR WARRIOR FAITH

The devil will do everything within his power to steal, kill and to destroy your family's faith in God (see John 10:10) and to steal the blessings of God to the third and fourth generations.

You are going to have to have the same kind of warrior faith that David showed when he and his militia of 600 men went to take back their families that the enemy had stolen. In 1 Samuel 30, we read about how David and his men returned from the land of the Philistines and came back to their camp at Ziklag. While they were away, their enemies, the Amalekites, came into their camp and raided and robbed them of everything, including their wives, their sons, their daughters and their possessions. The enemy stole their families just like Satan may have stolen your family, some of your material possessions and some of your spiritual heritage.

After he regrouped and regained his composure, David did exactly what a man of faith would do. He prayed and asked God for direction and for a specific word.

After you have surveyed the situation and regained your composure, the first step in using your faith to fight for your family is to *seek a specific Word from the Lord*. Your faith cannot be based on your feelings, your emotions, your anger, your displeasure, nor the need to or the feeling of getting even with someone. There is no other basis upon which you can rest your faith but the Word of God.

No matter how low you get; no matter how difficult the trial or how troubling the tribulation you and your family may be going through right now; no matter who rejects you or slanders you; no matter what has collapsed around you or what was stolen from you—God can and God will speak a Word to you. God will encourage you and strengthen you deep within your heart with a Word, a promise just for you—*if you will simply go to Him in prayer and sincerely seek His will and not your own.* You owe it to yourself as a father and you owe it to your family to be strong in the heat of every battle.

Secondly, you must now act in faith based on what God has said for your family. Look at what David did in verses 6-17—he acted in faith. He believed that what God said, God would do. God told David to go and attack and take back everything (all) that had been stolen. So David and the men with him immediately acted on the Word of God. Prayer will always be followed by action, because it is in the place of prayer that we discover our answers and our courage. Faith always acts on the Word of God. Faith does not hear the Word and then walk the other way. Faith acts on what God says in His Word and then allows God to produce and manage the results.

THE WORD OF GOD, NOT THE WORDS OF MEN, GUIDES FATHERS

One of the reasons so many families are in such disarray and are falling apart is because too many fathers are acting on what the news media say, what the economist says, what the negative prognosticators say, what grandma said and what the no-vision, low-vision person on the job said. Father, your family is in danger as long as you are governing your life and your family life based on what other people, other institutions and other so-called philosophers have to say rather than on a Word from the Lord God almighty, Maker of heaven and earth.

David and his men acted on the Word of God and overtook the enemy, and for one solid day and night whipped them up one side and down the other side. God is able to do exceedingly abundantly more than you can ask or think according to the power that works in you (the power that is at work in fathers is the father force and it is your faith) (see Ephesians 3:20), because this is the victory that overcomes the world—even our faith (see 1 John 5:4).

In verses 18-20 we see that God not only gave back their wives, their children and all their possessions, but He also gave them all the possessions of the enemy. They had more than they had lost!

If you are going to fight to save your family and use your faith to take back what belongs to you, father, you must determine that you are going to get up, stand up and show up for the fight and that you are going to go after your stolen property.

There comes a time in every father's and in every man's life when he must decide what he is going to do and who he is going to be. There comes a time when a father and a man, has to stand and having done all still stand and put on the whole armor of God (see Ephesians 6:13). Let me ask you, father, where are you? Are you at that point of desperation where you have decided that your son is not going to go the way of the rest of the crowd and that you just might have to stand up to the spirit of rebellion that you see developing a stronghold in him? Are you at the point of desperation where you have to stand up to the spirit of independence in your daughter and tell her that the skirt length in this house is where you say it is?

You are, at some point in time, going to have to stand and tell the devil, "No more!" And although as a father you may be talking to your spouse, your son or your daughter—remember that they are not the problem, nor the enemy…it is the spirit that is influencing them. Jesus had to stand up to his friend Peter and say, "Get behind Me, Satan, for you are concerned about the things of the world and not the things of the Father" (see Matthew 16:23).

A HERO'S PRAYER

No more—I am not going to sit here and feel sorry for myself. No more—I am not going to sit here and let you take my wife. I am not going to sit here and let you take my children, my finances, my health, my peace, my joy, my career, my mother, my brothers and my sisters. No more!

I am not going to let you take my calling to teach, my calling to worship, my potential, my passion, my gifts and my talents given to me by my God!

No more, Satan. You are going to give back my property, my stuff and my family. I come against you in the Name of Jesus Christ, and I plead the blood of Jesus against you and I resist you in the Name of Jesus Christ my Lord!

Remember, you are not engaged in natural, physical warfare. Fathers must stand up in the Spirit of Christ and step up and fight for their families with the weapons of prayer and faith.

Satan has no feelings of sympathy toward you. If you do not resist the devil, he will not flee from you—but will continue to steal, kill and destroy (see John 10:10) and rip you off every week, every month and every year.

BE ALL YOU CAN BE!

You do not have to be a victim. You can recover the faith the devil has stolen. You can recover everything that has ever been stolen from your family through prayer and faith. But you must believe that God is able to use you and that you can stand against the enemy, based on the Word of God. I am not talking about false faith that simply goes through the motions of prayer without power; praise that is plastic and phony; giving that is grievous; and a form of godliness that simply causes you to always come to church beat down and beat up and never victorious. That is a sure sign that you have lost faith in God's Word.

The faith that fights for the family and takes back what has been stolen is faith that is based on a Word from God and on the assurance that God will do it because He said it and because He is God. It is a faith in the living Lord Jesus Christ who came that you and your family might have life and have it more abundantly. I am talking about a faith in the King of kings who conquered Satan and who can and who will revive your marriage. It is Jesus who can and who will bring the joy back to your soul. It is Jesus who can and will renew your calling, recover your faith, re-ignite your passion and refocus your family on victory and not defeat; wealth and not poverty; hope and not failure. Jesus defeated Satan on behalf of your family. He made an open show of him and took away the keys to death, hell and the grave and gave you and your family the keys to the kingdom (see Matthew 16:19; Revelation 1:18).

My lesson of faith from George

Faith is the substance of things hoped for, the evidence of things not seen (Hebrews 11:1). Faith is also the ability to see the future in spite of the darkness of the present. George had that kind of faith. Times were changing. Sparky's Used Car Dealership where George had worked for years closed due to urban renewal and a proposed new highway. Competition began to discover that there was a future in collecting other people's garbage, and better-capitalized companies got into the trash collection business. George lost his clients.

Several neighbors had moved out and 12th Street was beginning to look abandoned. The corner grocery store closed down, and the talk was that our school, St. Paul's, would not reopen for the next semester.

George called our mother, Mamie, and they agreed that Tony, William, and I would move in with her. The day came and it was a cold, snowy day in Cincinnati, but it was also a bright day. George and Mamie agreed that we would all carry her last name, Davis, and that we would never refer to one another as "stepbrothers" or "stepsisters." As Mamie and Robert (our oldest brother) drove up to the apartment building, we could see them out of the third floor window. Tony and William were sad and down. I was excited. There was something in me that said we could do better and that we would see better days in the future—and we would rise above our circumstances.

I was the first one down the stairs and into the car. Tony, William and George came slowly and deliberately. After hugging our dad my brothers got in the back seat with me. George looked over at me, and I knew to get out of the car. When I did, he put his arms around me and walked me a few feet away from everyone and said, *"Phillip, don't look back, always believe in yourself and remember that you can accomplish anything because God is with you. Don't worry about me, I'll get another gig. I've got a plan to open a store near Middletown, and I want you to come see it when I have it ready. I love you."*

I have never forgotten the tenacious, persistent faith of my dad. It has been the one thing that keeps me going in the midst of difficult times. His faith in himself, in his God, and in me has helped me to endure hardships as a pastor, a husband, a father and a community servant. I later discovered in Romans 8:28 what I saw displayed in George's life. It says, *And we know that all things work together for good to those who love God, to those who are the called according to His purpose.* George did indeed get another gig. He did indeed open his store and continued to provide for his sons as best he could.

As a father you have a radical cause to instill faith in your children. You will need persistent faith because the enemy is trying to tempt you and pressure you to give up and to give out. But be not dismayed, God has not forsaken you. He has given you His Spirit to help you, empower you and enable you to reveal His presence and power in your home, your community, your church, and to advance His kingdom on earth as it is in heaven. The courage and wisdom that you find in the presence of the Father will be a great source of strength for your children. Never forget that God is your source and no matter how tough it gets, He will give you another "gig."

Heroes don't forget God

In the third chapter of Isaiah we discover a powerfully pointed and prophetic text. The situation was similar to that of our day and time. Israel was a sick nation with a morally corrupt society. They were people who had seen great prosperity (the best of times), and they enjoyed political prominence during the seventh and eighth centuries. Their economic prosperity and political power led them to forget about the God of their fathers. They forgot that it was God who had brought them out of bondage and who was the source of all their blessings. They bowed down and worshipped idols while oppressing the poor and neglecting the elderly, the widows and the orphans.

The nation of Israel had at one time walked closely with the Lord, but now they abused His sanctuary and entertained false prophets. They neglected to teach their children the Word and the ways of God, and they forgot to honor God in all their ways. They divorced their wives for any reason. They neglected their children, and on many occasions even sacrificed their children in the fire to the false Ammonite god called Molech, discussed in the books of Leviticus, First and Second Kings and also mentioned in Jeremiah.

As a result they became very corrupt. Violence, oppression and immorality swept the nation. The condition of the land and the hearts of the people, along with the immorality of its leadership, got so bad that God cried out to the prophet, *"And I looked, and there was no one to help, and I was astonished and there was no one to uphold..."* (Isaiah 63:5 NASB).

The nation suffered. The families of the land, the children and society as a whole suffered. The religious community suffered. The economy and all the land began to fail because God could not find one man [father] who would stand up and take his rightful place as His answer to the problems of society.

Fathers, our society, your family, community and church are all hurting and suffering and are on the brink of total destruction—unless God can count on you as a father to become one of the leaders in the land that He designed you to be.

In Isaiah 3:1-5, God says He will take away the supply and the support. When fathers refuse to lead and care for their families and take control of the culture, God says He will take away the food supply, the water and that which is used as staples in the economy.

In addition, God says He will take away the role models, the heroes, the warriors, the judges, prophets, elders, the counselors, skilled craftsmen, orators, and writers, men who are thinkers and men of rank or ability. Then, in verse 12, God says He will allow boys to become the officials and will allow the women and children to rule over the society. This seems to be more and more the condition of our culture.

As it was in the day of Isaiah's prophecy so it is today, people oppress one another. Brother fights against brother; sister against sister; neighbor against neighbor; and the young are rising up against the senior adults with contempt and disrespect. The base or low life has risen in rebellion against God-ordained authority. Why? Because when fathers refuse to lead, there can and will be no true leadership in the land.

The greatest problem in America and the world today is not that sinners are sinning. The greatest problem is that fathers are not leading and being the heroes who show their families a different way of life.

WHERE ARE THE HEROES?

The leadership that is needed will not and cannot come from the White House, from Congress, from the Supreme Court, from the Governor's Mansion or City Hall. The moral and spiritual leadership needed in our world today cannot come from those who do not know God. Regardless of their political affiliation, their position or rank—no matter what their party or what the opinion polls may say—God is looking for leadership from the ranks of Christian fathers.

The leadership we need is not going to come from sports superstars, Hollywood heroes or high profile entertainers. The leadership that will turn the hearts of fathers to their children, and the hearts of children to their fathers, and cause the land to be spared the wrath of God will come from those men of God—those fathers who understand the force and the power of fatherhood.

Fathers are the true heroes we are looking for. Fathers will inspire the next generation to fulfill their destiny. I have often wondered why I have never been *"star struck"* or been able to comfortably acknowledge another man as my hero. I questioned myself and examined my motives and even confessed pride and selfishness.

However, what the Spirit of God has helped me to see is that the reason I could not acknowledge other men as my heroes is because I had not acknowledged the man who shaped my life and instilled the virtues, qualities and will to succeed in my life. I had not, until then, acknowledged the true hero in my life, the man who helped shape my destiny and propel me with the force of fatherhood, my dad, George. My father is my hero.

FATHER REFLECTIONS

1. *What has the enemy stolen from you and your family that you need to reclaim?*

2. *How strong and how persistent is your faith?*

3. *Who is your hero? How does this person exemplify the characteristics of a courageous leader?*

4. *How can you, as a father, help put others in remembrance of the promises of God?*

CHAPTER EIGHT

Father—Why Is His Decision Making So Critical?

"He is our decisive dad."

God desires to bless your family as well as all the families of the earth. In Genesis 12:1-3, God declares that He will bless your family so that your family might be a blessing to some other family.

Although it is God's desire to bless your family and make it a strong and healthy representation of His presence in the earth today, God cannot and will not act contrary to His Word. God cannot act contrary to His laws. Psalm 119:89 says, *Forever, O Lord, Your word is settled in heaven.* When you and your family are out of line with the known will of God and the revealed Word of God, God is not being cruel, harsh or acting against His nature when He allows the natural consequences of your choices to come to pass.

Because of His mercy and grace, God will forgive us and give us another chance to grow strong families and build healthy relationships. However, we must do our part and diligently obey Him. Although there seems to be a deterioration of the family structure, I believe that we have many, and can have many more, strong families. In order to do so, it is critical that fathers, particularly, stop allowing newspapers and the nightly media pundits to tell us how bad we are, how hopeless we are, and how dysfunctional we all are.

Father, you are created in the image and likeness of the heavenly Father, God, and as His representatives in the earth, you must begin and continue to say what God says about you. Also, you must choose to allow your life to be transformed by a renewing of your mind, rearranging the way you think. *Do not be conformed to this world, but be transformed by the renewing of your mind...* (Romans 12:2). God said in His Word that we have been "adopted into His family," and God's family is not dysfunctional. God's family is complete, whole, blessed and anointed with the power to change the world.

God has done, and is doing, His part. He is faithful and we can depend on Him. The key, then, is for you and me, as fathers in the earth, to do our part in redeeming the land and growing strong families. I believe that it all starts with fathers who understand the force of fatherhood.

FATHER FROM THE INSIDE OUT

Today, more than ever, we need fathers who are men of courage and conviction. Our children need decisive dads—fathers who can, and will, make decisions and stick by them. We must have fathers who will make, or who have made, some very basic decisions about who they are and what they are going to do and about what the standards will be in their households.

> *If there are no universal recipes, no quick-fix formulas for parents and fathers; if answers, such as they are, are as much based on who one is as they are on what one does, then what in heaven's name must a man do if he is to become a better, indeed, a good father?* [7]

Your actions as a father proceed from who you are in your core being. The decisions you make for you and your family will be founded on your core being. If you simply try to make better decisions and act better as a father, without changing your inside, there will always be a struggle. The power for father force comes from within. If there are insecurities, psychological angst, internal pain, unforgiveness and unresolved conflict, guilt or shame, your decision making power will be weakened. Inferior forces from within will be guiding you and resisting your perspective and resolution.

Father, you can never behave for an extended period of time in a manner that is inconsistent with the way you see yourself. Your internal self-concept, your being, will always produce your doing.

As you give yourself to the changing power of the Spirit, allowing your mind and spirit to be healed and reshaped, this transforming power will liberate you to

---

[7] Mark O'Connell, *The Good Father*, (Scribner, New York, 2005) 171.

become who you need to be and to do what you need to do. Learning to father from within can only become effective when the interior "you" has been healed and is controlled by the Spirit of God. In order to make clear, decisive, correct and Spirit-filled decisions, the inner child must put away childish things and become a man.

THE STEPS TO BECOMING A MAN

Human understanding tells us that becoming a man is simply a matter of growing a strong body. We live in a culture that puts too much focus on the exterior body. We are surrounded by this cultural invasion into our spiritual privacy. Being bombarded by commercials, movies, and billboards, we are tempted to succumb to this false advertising. Too many Christian men are being conditioned by culture and society to define themselves according to the world's standards rather than according to the Word of God. As a result, too many Christian fathers and Christian men are not enjoying the privilege and power of being a man.

God has a better plan. You can know and acknowledge God's plan and purpose for becoming a man and recognize that manhood is wonderful. It is great, it is valuable and it can be enjoyable. This new realization will begin when you understand that becoming a man does not begin in the gym but begins in your inner soul. It is not instantaneous. It is a journey.

MANHOOD IS NOT A DESTINATION; IT IS A JOURNEY...MANHOOD IS A PART OF THE NEVER-ENDING JOURNEY CALLED LIFE.

Whether you are twenty-five or fifty-five years of age, you need to declare a point in your life, mark it by some unmistakable ceremony, and announce to your wife, your family, your church, and your friends—*"This is it, I am crossing over right here and right now."* Once you have made the decision, the choice to become a man will depend on your walking in obedience to the Word and the will of God and the Spirit of God as you travel the pathway of life. For a boy to become a man he must first break free from his mother and find his father. Many men have never broken free of their mothers, thus they have never found their fathers who can lead them into manhood. There are many who can teach you, but there are few who can father you. Only fathers can teach you to become a father. Paul understood this principle.

> *I write not these things to shame you, but as my beloved sons I warn you. For though ye have ten thousand instructors in Christ, yet have ye not many fathers: for in Christ Jesus I have begotten you through the gospel. Wherefore I beseech you, be ye followers of me.*
> —1 Corinthians 4:14-16 KJV

To become a man you must master the child within. Within every man dwells the little child who preceded him.

> *When I was a child, I used to speak as a child, think as a child, reason as a child; when I became a man, I did away with childish things.*
> —1 Corinthians 13:11 NASB

Whether you know it or not, that little child is speaking to you every day and guiding you. But in order to become a man you must allow yourself to transcend the inner child.

"I spoke as a child..."

Did you really speak as a child? Many men lose their ability to communicate during childhood, and it affects them negatively for the rest of their lives. They become biological fathers with a child's verbal communication level. In many men, the child was not allowed to speak, but rather the child was silenced by abuse, neglect and ridicule. He was never allowed to express himself, and when the child became a man the inner child did not grow up. He is still affected by the inward child who was silenced and never learned to talk. Because he does not know how to talk, he is restricted in his decision-making ability as a man.

> And it came about that after three days they found Him in the temple, sitting in the midst of the teachers, both listening to them, and asking them questions.
> —Luke 2:46 NASB

As a child, Jesus could sit among men and interact with them. His voice was being developed right there in the middle of those religious leaders. Self-expression is key to decision making, and when it is impeded in earlier years, it will have adverse effects in later years. Developing the ability to reason and think through issues is a lifetime process, and we often have to overcome the earlier consequences of our childhood.

Fathers, if you are having a difficult time communicating with your wives or your children, it could very well be because you did not get the opportunity to speak as a child.

Regardless of the past, you can do something about it today. You can declare your freedom from the past by saying with the apostle Paul, *…forgetting what lies behind and reaching forward to what lies ahead, I press on toward the goal for the prize of the upward call of God in Christ Jesus* (Philippians 3:13-14 NASB).

"I understood as a child…"

Many fathers today are making childish decisions because in many ways they are still children. You can only be young once, but you can be immature for a lifetime. What is normal for a child can be deadly for a man who still understands as a child. If your understanding is disabled and does not mature, your ability to make decisions will remain retarded. The writer of Proverbs 4:7 says, *"Wisdom is the principal thing; therefore get wisdom. And in all your getting, get understanding."*

Paradigms and mindsets established in our earlier years are hard to overcome in our adult years. Mature fathers and men are able to transcend and rise above those childish mindsets and recreate new paradigms for a new world.

"I thought as a child…"

The minds of children should not be stressed with harsh issues like molestation, abuse, or domestic violence. Can you imagine the thoughts that go through the minds of children who have to suffer this type of life? When you understand as a child—you think as a child.

The signs of mature thinking are evident in fathers who are able to reflect, imagine, search out truth, and work through issues and problems. They are able to push aside emotions and insecurities and work through the problem as they seek a determined resolution.

What should we do? How do we put away childish things and become a man? Jesus said, ... *"Suffer the little children to come unto me, and forbid them not: for of such is the kingdom of God"* (Mark 10:14 KJV). The enemy is within and the answer is also within. You can never become the man you want to be and the man God can use until you can put away the man you used to be and develop the man you are right now.

If you want to be free, challenge all the world's standards and definitions of manhood and acknowledge God's plan and pattern of manhood. Growth is neither cheap nor easy. It will cost you a *death to the old self* in order to experience the *birth of the new man*, who after Christ is created in true righteousness and holiness (see Ephesians 4:24).

How do you know when you have put away childish things and become a man?

First, you must learn how to celebrate your masculinity. You become proud to be a man after God's own heart (see Acts 13:22; 1 Samuel 13:14). You need a heart transplant, something that is only possible by the Spirit. A father with God's heart will reflect God's mind and character. Father, you must refuse to be restricted by fleshly, selfish attitudes and rejoice in the fact that the heart of God controls your life.

Secondly, you recognize that God is the source of your strength. A real father and man realizes that his strength comes from knowing his God. Daniel 11:32 says, *"...the people who know their God shall be strong, and carry out great exploits."*

> *David said moreover,* **The LORD that delivered me** *out of the paw of the lion, and out of the paw of the bear, he will deliver me out of the hand of this Philistine. And Saul said unto David, Go, and the LORD be with thee. And Saul armed David with his armour, and he put an helmet of brass upon his head; also he armed him with a coat of mail. And David girded his sword upon his armour, and he assayed to go; for he had not proved it. And David said unto Saul, I cannot go with these; for I have not proved them. And David put them off him. And he took his staff in his hand, and chose him five smooth stones out of the brook, and put them in a shepherd's bag which he had, even in a scrip; and his sling was in his hand: and he drew near to the Philistine.*
> —1 Samuel 17:37-40 KJV
> (Emphasis added)

As fathers, we must understand that our strength does not come from fleshly means but from the Lord. We must understand that we cannot arise to our great potential unless we have learned to connect to our inward spiritual power that comes from the Lord.

Being strong does not mean that you are not sensitive. You can develop the ability to be tenderhearted, sensitive, and affectionate and still be strong, tough and a warrior in battle. Fathers must learn how to walk the tightrope between being a lion and being a lamb. Only the Holy Spirit can give you the true balance that all men seek.

More than any other man, Jesus demonstrated perfect balance in the duplex nature of a man. He showed us the perfect pattern of holistic masculinity. Far too many children are suffering because their fathers have never decided to lead them in the right direction, to be the role models and the examples of manhood to them, to teach them about their spiritual heritage and to share with them the knowledge of God.

BEING A DECISIVE DAD

Joshua was a decisive dad. He was a man whom God had used greatly to lead the nation of Israel into the Promised Land. Joshua, in the 24th chapter of the book that bears his name, was old and the Bible says he was well stricken in years. Joshua wanted to give the people one last word of warning before he went the way of men. So he gathered the people of the nation before him and reviewed and reflected on the goodness and the faithfulness of God toward them. Then Joshua brought the people to the point of commitment and told them to make a choice—decide, choose, and commit once and for all whom you will serve.

Joshua was not calling for a temporary commitment, rather, a once and for all, total, complete, and definite decision to follow the ways of God. Joshua set the pace by declaring his position and that of his family—"...*But as for me and my house, we will serve the Lord*" (Joshua 24:15). Joshua showed us the value of a father who is decisive and the difference that father makes in his home, his community and his church.

First, Joshua was decisive in his leadership. One of the saddest sights in the world is a father who has no guts, no backbone, and no courage to be the leader in his home. God created the man and gave him the honored and privileged position of leadership, and because it is an assignment from God, father, you are accountable to God for how you lead your family. The Bible says that the gifts and the calling of God are without repentance (see Romans 11:29).

Although leadership is not something you can *demand*, it is something you can *command* by your godly lifestyle and by your tender treatment of your wife and children. Too many fathers want to demand respect and demand leadership in their homes. The problem with demanding respect is that those in your home may comply, but they will never be committed to your leadership. That is, not until you decide to be the kind of leader that represents the servanthood of Christ.

Joshua was so decisive about what he and his family were going to do, because he was a father who was the respected leader. His family respected his decisions because they had seen his faithfulness and witnessed his dependability over the years. They had witnessed his consistent lifestyle and therefore they gave him the respect he was due.

Secondly, Joshua made a decision to be consistent. Fathers, you have been given the privilege to lead and give direction to your wives and children. However, if you, as a father are living a trashy and inconsistent lifestyle with cursing, drinking, smoking, lying, pornography, and other personal vices, you will never be able to be the decisive dad that your family needs you to be. If you, as a father, speak down and verbally or emotionally abuse your children or wife, you temporarily forfeit your privilege to lead until you repent and demonstrate that you can and are willing to be a decisive dad.

Joshua lived a consistently godly lifestyle before his family. Therefore, he could boldly declare, "As for me and my house...."

Joshua was his children's hero and his wife's knight in shining armor. He was so consistent in his lifestyle that his children needed no one else to be their role model. It is vital that you do not allow your children to hold up so-called celebrities or sports stars as role models. Proverbs 17:6 KJV says, *"...the glory of children are their fathers."*

Dads who are decisive about living a consistently godly life are to be the role models, the heroes and the ones who are looked to by the children and the families of the world. As you are consistent in your commitments to your family, consistent in your commitments to your church, consistent in your love toward your wife and consistent in your Bible study, prayer and worship, you will demonstrate that God our Father is consistent and that He can be depended upon.

Finally, Joshua was decisive about being a public witness to the goodness of God. Father, it is time to go public with your faith and to begin sharing with other fathers and other men, your witness and your testimony of the love and the grace of God in your life. We have far too many *stealth* fathers who want to be Christians on Sunday yet never have a word to say about their relationship with Jesus Christ during the rest of the week. We have too many secret agent fathers who claim to be Christians but are not willing to live for Christ publicly.

Our children are ashamed of their faith because many of them have never heard their fathers bear witness to their faith in a public fashion. Fathers, God saved you so you could go public and let other fathers, other men, know that you and your family, you and your house, are servants of the Lord.

Joshua made a decision to go public. Joshua went public, and he told all the people, the young and the old, the rich and the poor, the concerned and the unconcerned, that he and his household loved God and that they were going to serve the God whom they loved. Joshua was willing to witness, and the Lord is still calling and looking for fathers who are not ashamed of the gospel of Jesus Christ.

Until you go into the business community, the halls of government, the legal system, the entertainment world, the sports world, the economic world, the education world, and even into the world of vices and vicissitudes, and declare publicly your allegiance to the Lord God of Heaven and earth, you will never be able to motivate your children to be totally committed to their faith in Christ.

Joshua spoke openly and plainly for all to hear, without any hesitation, reservation or fear of retaliation. *As for me and my wife; as for me and my children; as for me and my money; as for me and all that is within me and under me and given to me by God—we shall serve the Lord.*

God is looking for decisive dads; bold fathers who will be witnesses unto Him. God is looking for fathers who are willing to stand and, having done all still stand against the gates of hell and the powers of darkness, to take back the streets of the city; take back our homes in the land; take back the halls of the schools and the minds of our wives and children.

A NEW FATHER FORCE IN THE EARTH

Never before in the history of the world have we been as much in need of the father force as we are at this moment. When God created fathers, he gave them the responsibility to be the visionary leader who would lead mankind into having dominion over the entire earth. Fathers were given the responsibility to be protectors, providers, priests and the spiritual direction and identity for their children and their children's children.

Men in general have been lacking in their understanding of the powerful force of fatherhood. Statistics today show us a society with an alarming trend toward deterioration. Marriages are failing, parents are absent, and children are paying the emotional, the financial, the physical and the spiritual consequences.

It is the breakdown of the family that is at the root of much of the economic and social instability. Nearly two out of every five children in America do not live with their fathers. Fatherlessness is the most destructive trend in our generation.

If the hearts of fathers are not restored and returned to their children, both naturally and spiritually, then Malachi 4:6 says that the Lord will "...*strike the earth with a curse*." When fathers are out of position and out of their place of spiritual, moral and natural leadership; when the relationship between the generations is estranged, they become cursed. God repeatedly said that He was the **"God of Abraham, of Isaac and of Jacob"** throughout the Old and New Testaments. He always referred to Himself in terms of generations of father to son and to his son's son.

God is calling fathers to become the force for stability, the force of strength and the force of security in the lives of their children and their wives. A father is called to be a protector, a provider, a priest and a person of decision for his children to follow.

Fathers are called to lead, and in this day and time God is calling you and me, as fathers, to become the leaders in every area of society so our children will be left with a legacy and a heritage, a foundation upon which to build their lives and the lives of their children.

On June 3, 1994, George died of a massive blood clot in his leg as he left the University of Cincinnati Medical Center after being treated for asthma. He suffered with asthma for as long as I can remember.

On Wednesday, June 8, 1994 at 7:00 p.m., I preached my dad's funeral. I also caught his spirit of fatherhood that changed my world and that is my driving passion to this day. His force as a father now lives in me. It is my desire to so impact my family by the decisions I make, that I can be the father force for them and so that they can be a force in their generation.

FATHER REFLECTIONS

1. *In what ways are you following the "inner child"?*

2. *How can your relationship with Christ and the Holy Spirit help you to become the man God designed you to be?*

3. *Are you a man like Joshua—full of character, courage and conviction? Why or why not?*

4. *How have your decisions as a father affected your children and family?*

A RADICAL REVOLUTION AGAINST FATHERHOOD

I don't know about you, but I am a bit weary of the world portraying and depicting fathers as weak, mindless, indecisive, impotent perverts on one hand and unfaithful, irresponsible, abusive gigolos on the other hand. I refuse to believe and accept the world's unfriendly portraits and negative stereotypes, which are nothing more than a satanically induced, radical revolution against the real power and godly influence that we as fathers and men have in this world.

Satan understands that if fathers and men truly accepted their God-given role and walked in their God-given power, the *Father Force* for good, righteousness, justice and peace would be so overwhelming that the underground economies of the drug trade, the prostitution trade, the gambling industry, the pornography industry, the abortion, tobacco and alcohol industries would dry up in a short period of time.

Satan understands that if fathers and men truly knew their identity and the power of their unity, the *Father Force* of holiness and godliness would drive out the spirit of violence from our schools; the spirit of rebellion from our homes; the spirit of lust, greed and wickedness from the corporate boardrooms as well as drive out the spirit of feminism and homosexuality from our communities.

It is because he understands the power of the *Father Force*, and the power of men committed to Christ and the Kingdom of God, that our enemy is so persistent in leading this relentless war, this radical revolution against fatherhood. This war to destroy the value, the dignity and the authority of fathers and men is being waged in the media through movies, television sitcoms, radio, the Internet, magazines and the various news outlets. Fathers, husbands and men in general are being depicted as unloving, cold, distant, uncaring, unfeeling *...lovers of pleasure rather than lovers of* [family and] *God* (2 Timothy 3:4). This is a real war with the radical agenda to destroy the very heart of fathers and men. We must resist it, fight it and overcome it—by any means necessary!

THE RADICAL CAUSE FOR FATHERHOOD

Just as there is a radical revolution against fatherhood, we have a radical cause for which to fight! If we as fathers and men were not a threat; if we were not the answer to the challenges, the problems, the sin and the wickedness of society, we would not be the major targets of the enemy's attack. I am not naive to the fact that there are fathers who are abusive, neglectful, reckless and generally trifling. I understand that there are some men who claim to be men, but who do not understand what it means to be a man, nor do they know how to conduct themselves as representatives of the God who created them.

I understand that there are some absentee, deadbeat dads, molesters of their children, and there are some men who beat their wives. And, yes, there are some men who are so vile and wicked they are worth nothing more than to be fuel for the fire of hell.

However, that type of father, that type of man, represents only a small percentage, only a small portion, only a small minority of fathers and men. While very few, if any of us, are *ideal* fathers or *perfect* fathers and men, I believe that most are trying to do what is right toward their children and their wives. I believe that most fathers and men want to do what is right. Most fathers work hard to bring home a living and to care for their families. Most are seeking to raise a righteous seed and prepare for their children's future. Most seek to discipline out of love and not to punish out of anger. Most are willing to learn, to try and to make some degree of change for the betterment of their families. Most are faithful to their spouse, devoted to their children and concerned about their community.

We have a radical cause. We have something to celebrate—the power of the *Father Force!*

THE RADICAL POWER OF FATHERHOOD

I believe in fatherhood and the radical power that God has given to fathers and to men. I believe that we should celebrate fathers and not have to wait for, or take our cue from, the world.

Men and fathers, you are the apple of God's eye (see Zechariah 2:8), and you are His chosen and handpicked agents of dominion and authority. *You are a chosen generation, a royal priesthood, a holy nation, His own special people, that you may proclaim the praises of Him who called you out of darkness into His marvelous light* (1 Peter 2:9). You are God's ambassador in the earth!

You must understand that your role and your responsibility are awesome and wonderful in the sight of God. Whether you are a biological father, an adoptive father, a stepfather, a surrogate father or a spiritual father like Paul mentions in 1 Corinthians 4:15, you must understand that you will need the power of fatherhood to deal with the radical nature of the enemy against you and your family. I have an acronym for *FATHER* that I want to share with you because I believe it will help you understand the power of fatherhood and the father force.

F—THE POWER OF FAITH

> *Take the first step in faith. You don't have to see the whole staircase, just take the first step.*
> —Dr. Martin Luther King, Jr.

Fathers have to ...*walk by faith, not by sight* (2 Corinthians 5:7). It is the power of your faith that will keep your wife calm, your children collected and your family moving forward. You have to be a father and man of powerful faith, who dreams dreams and sees visions of a better tomorrow. When no one else in the family is dreaming, when no one else has a vision, you, as the father, must have the faith to have a clear vision of the preferable future. You have to walk in the power of faith that allows you and your family to live victorious today and envision living even better tomorrow.

Don't wait on your wife to pray...you pray. You might have to pray by yourself. You might have to tell God, *"God, they think that I am strong. They think I've got it together...but I am hurting and I am afraid, and if You, Lord, don't move in our home…if You don't show Yourself mighty in our finances, I don't know what I am going to do.*"After you pray, you get up as the father and stand up as the man, and begin walking by faith, knowing that if God be for you, who can be against you (see Romans 8:31).

A—THE POWER OF ADAPTABILITY

Adaptability is not imitation. It means power of resistance and assimilation.
—Mahatma Gandhi

Fathers, you must have a plan. You must have goals, dreams and vision. But don't limit yourself and don't limit your children to reaching the goal by traveling one way. Understand that many are the plans of men—but the ways of God stand sure! (see Proverbs 19:21). If life throws you a detour, don't give up on your goals for your family and your children. If life causes you to change lanes, then change lanes, but just keep headed in the right direction. Be adaptable, adjustable and flexible. The apostle Paul said, …*I have become all things to all men, that I might by all means save some* (1 Corinthians 9:22).

Fathers, be adaptable. Don't be so rigid and unbending that you can't allow for new things and new ways of getting things done. Your children are learning differently than you learned. They are experimenting with and mastering technology that you and I have not been exposed to. Accept, acknowledge and adjust to that which is new—just as long as you do not adjust or compromise the message of truth and your standards of holiness and righteousness.

T—THE POWER OF TIMING

Life is all about timing...the unreachable becomes reachable, the unavailable become available, the unattainable...attainable. Have the patience, wait it out. It's all about timing.

—Stacey Charter

As a father, let me assure you that there are some things that only time can take care of. You thought your son would never come to his senses, but time took care of him. You might think that your daughter will never understand and never follow after the principles of life and living that you taught her, but hold on, father. There is a thing called time. Time will be the great equalizer. If you learn to wait on the Lord and be of good courage, not only will He strengthen your heart, but you will see the goodness of the Lord in the land of the living (see Psalm 27:13-14).

H—THE POWER OF HUMILITY

Do you wish to rise? Begin by descending. You plan a tower that will pierce the clouds? Lay first the foundation of humility.

—Saint Augustine

I don't care how well you are doing, how much bacon you bring home and how well off your family may be. Father, you must understand that it is only as you ...*walk humbly with your God* (Micah 6:8), and it is only as you ...*humble yourselves under the mighty hand of God* (1 Peter 5:6), that you will be able to sustain the blessings and honor and favor of God upon your children and your children's children.

No man is a self-made man. God gave you what you have and God provided for your needs. You are what you are, by the grace of God (see 1 Corinthians 15:10). It is only through the power of humility that you can teach your children how to totally depend on the Lord. You are going to have to trust the power of humility. Humility means that you can cast your cares on God, knowing that He cares for you. Humility is admitting that there are some things that are beyond your ability to control and that you need God to handle them. Walk humbly with your God.

E—THE POWER OF EXCELLENCE

I just try to be the best I can be and hope that is the best ever.
    —Tiger Woods, professional golfer

Fathers must serve their families, their churches and their communities in the power of excellence. The Bible teaches that, as a father, you are created a little lower than God (see Psalm 8:5). God has given you as fathers and men, dominion over the earth and every creeping thing and beast of the field (see Genesis 1:28).

As a father, you are the authority of God in the earth today. With that responsibility also comes the accountability to do all things well and to do them with a *spirit of excellence.*

Excellence does not mean perfection—there will never be another perfect man other than the Man, Christ Jesus. Excellence means that you as a father never settle for less than your personal best and that you reflect that spirit of excellence in front of your children.

The psalmist says in Psalm 8:1, "*O Lord, Our Lord, how excellent is Your name in all the earth....*"

R—THE POWER OF RIGHTEOUSNESS

"But seek ye first the kingdom of God, and his right-eousness; and all these things shall be added unto you."

—Jesus Christ
—Matthew 6:33 KJV

Fathers must understand the power of their righteousness. To those fathers who have been born again, 2 Corinthians 5:17 says, *...old things have passed away; behold, all things have become new.* You are no longer a failure as a father. You may stumble and you may fall, but as the righteousness of God in Christ (see Romans 3:22), you have the power to get up again and to continue moving toward the divine destiny to which God has called you—to become the image of Christ in the eyes of your children and spouse.

The world will make every attempt to beat you down and to cast you out as a no good, worthless and useless father. The world will try to convince you that since you have not been the ideal or the perfect father, that you are disqualified from being the role model to your son or daughter. However, God is not looking for perfect fathers. God is looking for fathers who are willing to be molded, shaped and transformed into the image of Christ.

Never misunderstand and never accept the lie from the enemy that your identity as a father is determined by your performance as a father or as a man. Your identity is not determined by your performance—your identity is determined by your birth. If you have been born again into the family of God, you are a saved, sanctified, son of God. You might not cross every "t" and you may not dot every "i," but God is a good Father and He … *"will never leave you nor* [will He] *forsake you* (Hebrews 13:5).

When you understand that you are in a right relationship with the Redeemer based solely on His mercy and grace, then you, as a father, can walk in a right relationship with your wife, with your children, with your church, and with your community based on mercy and grace. Father, you are the hope of the next generation.

You are the father force that will change the world.

APPENDIX

PHILLIP M. DAVIS MINISTRIES
Live Today, Envision Tomorrow

THE FATHER FORCE

"And he will restore the hearts of the fathers to their children, and the hearts of the children to their fathers, lest I come and smite the land with a curse."
—Malachi 4:6 NASB

OUR MISSION

The Father Force®, was born of the Spirit out of the heart of Bishop Phillip M. Davis to meet the need for positive affirmation and biblical equipping in the lives of fathers in particular and men in general.

The Father Force® therefore exists to both equip and encourage men to be better fathers and men of godly character who see themselves as agents of godly change in our culture.

OUR VISION

It is the vision of The Father Force® to be a catalyst for change in the lives of men around the world and to be a resource center for equipping and training men in their God-given roles as prophets, priests, protectors, providers and pals (friends) to their wives, their children, their churches and their communities.

OUR STRATEGY

The Father Force® will use every available medium of communication to be the catalyst of change in the lives of fathers and men worldwide. We will employ the use of conferences, workshops, small groups, personal appearances, television, radio and the Internet to reach fathers and men for the purpose of equipping and encouraging them in their destiny.

For more information contact:

The Father Force®
Post Office Box 77285
Charlotte, NC 28277
1-800-887-8850
www.thefatherforce.org
www.phillipdavisministries.org
www.nationsford.org

ABOUT THE AUTHOR

Phillip M. Davis is the founding pastor of Nations Ford Community Church of Charlotte, NC. Bishop Davis and his wife, Cynthia, also founded the Galilean Baptist Church of Charlotte, the Alpha Community Church of Alpharetta, GA and have led their ministry to assist in the establishment and development of over a dozen other churches of various racial and ethnic backgrounds.

A graduate of Xavier University of Cincinnati, Ohio and of The Carolina University of Theology, Bishop Davis has served in leadership capacities with the North American Mission Board, SBC; the Columbia International University and is the founder of the Queen City Bible College of Charlotte, NC.

Bishop Davis is the presiding Bishop of Community Church Network, founded to encourage and equip church planters and church leaders who are in the transition of moving from traditional to contemporary leadership and worship.

He is married to his high school sweetheart, Cynthia, and together they have been serving in ministry for over 26 years and have been married for more than 32 years. The Davises are the very proud parents of three grown children, Minister R.J. Davis (Kim) of Long Beach, CA; Ashley Hall (Jay) and Bradley Davis. They have one gorgeous grand-daughter, Jada Hall.

Bishop Davis and Cynthia are pastors to pastors, serving as spiritual father and mother to many. They have given themselves in service to the Body of Christ as spiritual parents, preaching and teaching the necessity for the spirit of fatherhood to be returned to our homes, churches and communities.